More Praise for

Your Mind Is What Matters
By Ivy Chin

"Having been part of Ivy's team in the past, I've experienced her mentoring firsthand. From the ABC's of prioritization to the Rule of Three, applying these actions will free the mind of clutter in order to focus on the desired outcome. If you are starting out your career or simply just need to recalibrate yourself, this book is an essential guidepost on the journey to maintaining a positive mind."

— *Heather Teasley*
Director of eCommerce, Mitchell Gold + Bob Williams

"Your Mind Is What Matters by Ivy Chin is smart, funny and packed full of valuable practices and techniques. The reader is brought into her life to see her resilience, strength and ultimate desire to be the best version of herself, improving humanity along the way. Her ability to honestly reflect on her choices and experiences is inspiring to those who are still in the early stages of knowing themselves and making their first steps forward into adult and working life."

— *Gina Neeley*
Homesteader

"Ivy writes of her journey of a young girl that transformed into a young lady after traveling to the United States overcoming immense odds and challenges with tenacity and determination. She takes the reader on an amazing education and corporate journey that transformed her life and perspective. Finally, Ivy provides a road-map, advice and insight on how a person can navigate their challenges."

— Regina D. Campbell, Ph.D.
Campus Dean

"How did a young teenager leave her family in Taiwan, travel to America, and rise through the ranks of corporate America? Ivy Chin not only shares her cultural challenges, but also, encapsulates her life lessons along the way of this incredible journey! A must read for those of us in the pursuit of happiness in our personal and professional lives."

— Steve Hamlin
Retired CEO - Commerce Hub

Your
MIND
Is What
MATTERS

How to Think Your Way to Your Full Potential

IVY CHIN

Maxurpo Publishing

This book may be purchased for business, education, or non-profit use. For details please email ichin@maxurpo.com

Book design by:
Arbor Services, Inc.

Printed in the United States of America

Your Mind Is What Matters
Ivy Chin

1. Self-Help. 2. Life Skills. 3. Personal Transformation.
4. Business Skills. I. Chin, Ivy. II. Title. III. Title: How to think your way to your full potential

Library of Congress Control Number: 2018904663
ISBN 13: 978-0-692-10680-8

"The will to win, the desire to succeed, the urge to reach your full potential... these are the keys that will unlock the door to personal excellence."

— Confucius

Contents

Chapter One

Your Mind Has the Power.. 1

Chapter Two

Think About the Positive End 7

Chapter Three

Know Your Strengths, Find Your Passion........................ 19

Chapter Four

Put Down the Baggage 33

Chapter Five

Where There's a Will, There's a Way 45

Chapter Six

Priority Is Productivity 55

Chapter Seven

Balance Traditions, Conditions, and Faith..................... 65

Chapter Eight

Manage Perception and Your Brand 75

Chapter Nine

Live Like There's No Tomorrow 87

Chapter Ten

Your Journey Is Ahead of You 97

About the Author.. 101

Chapter One

Your Mind Has the Power

All I could think about was what we would eat for lunch. My fellow students were more diverse in their interests. Nancy was a smart girl, but she neglected her studies. Just like always before a big test, she bent over the math book lying open on her desk, trying to cram in material at the last minute. Brenda, who had already decided at age thirteen that her future did not include advanced algebra, was reading a comic.

This was the heyday of Japanese manga in my native Taiwan. Kids my age especially loved the imported books. I was a fan too, but my parents didn't approve. A friend introduced me to a story involving a young girl who went back in time to ancient Egypt and fell in love with the prince. I used to daydream about taking her place. Brenda took her interest to a much higher level. I never saw her crack her textbook except when the teacher's eyes were on her. At all other times, her attention was glued to the black-and-white romance stories with their translated Mandarin text.

I was more serious about school subjects than Brenda, but not because I loved learning. That love had been squeezed out of me long before I was a teenager. Hours spent repeating lessons that the teacher chanted in monotone exhausted all interest I had in understanding math, science, history, or literature. Schoolwork didn't consist of anything to understand, just lists of facts to put in my head, then dump out onto the exam papers that checked our memorization skills every day. I had already taken three exams on the day in question, and was "looking forward" to three more before school ended. I'd given up hope of pulling off any last-minute miracles when it came to my test scores. I would score well in math, earning praise from my parents if not my teacher. Mine would not be top marks, but I would leave Brenda's score far behind, with many more of my classmates envious of my achievement.

Many of my recollections of the Taiwanese school system are vague, more impressions than concrete memories. What I do remember was the emphasis on facts, facts, facts. Learn some facts, take a test. Learn more facts, take another test. As a kid, it seemed to me that the purpose of today's facts was to get me through tomorrow's tests. The pressure to do well in my subjects, combined with the way they were taught, made it impossible to see classwork as anything more than a means to an end. My fellow students and I were expected to be human calculators, reading questions and flashing back answers from our bright eyes. The teachers showed us mountains of information, but they never equipped us with the tools we needed to dig out meaning.

Having been educated in the US, my parents had definite views on what they wanted their daughter to learn. Mom and Dad both told me from an early age that I could be one of two things when

I grew up: a doctor or an engineer. My test scores said that I was a good student, but as Dad watched me labor at my studies night after night, his suspicions grew that I didn't truly understand what I was learning. I must acknowledge his insight with respect and gratitude. All during my childhood, he had monitored my progress as a student. One night, he decided he'd seen enough. Seating me in front of him, he began to ask me questions, probing the inner truths of lessons my tests said I had learned well. It didn't take long for him to expose my limitations. My knowledge was broad as oceans, shallow as foam. Something had to change.

The solution Dad explained to me that night was that I would attend junior high and high school in the States, in preparation for entering medical or engineering school. I took this pronouncement in stride. As a teenager, the idea of moving to a different country sounded cool. I thought making new friends would be easy. Getting more out of my school time was a bonus. It's worth mentioning that my favorite food at the time was corn dogs. America, the birthplace of that deep-fried delicacy, sounded like a grand adventure.

The move was brave for Mom and Dad. They knew their traditional ideas of how my life should play out would be challenged. I've always been impressed that having seen the finish line they wanted me to reach, they didn't stand idle while I finished in the middle of the pack. Instead, they pointed out a different road where I had a chance to take the lead. At the time, I didn't fully appreciate their sacrifice, but that didn't stop me from doing my best. I dreaded, as the daughter of an Asian household, doing anything that might cause the family to lose face.

The challenge of going to school in America proved greater than I'd anticipated. I had taken English classes in Taiwan, and though I was not as good in languages as I was in mathematics, I thought I was good enough. Soon after arriving on US soil, I found that expressing myself was a huge problem. The words and phrases I had practiced for years didn't fit most situations. Getting across the simplest thoughts was as frustrating as any test I'd taken at my old school.

Did I recoil from this unexpected difficulty? Maybe it would be more dramatic to say I did. But honestly, as best I can remember, I never considered throwing up my hands. Mom wasn't about to send me back to Taiwan, so what would have been the point? Frustration didn't make me want to quit. It made me want to find a solution. Maybe that's part of having a mathematical mind. I firmly believe all problems can be solved if you apply the power of your mind. Up to that point in my life, Mom and Dad had smoothed the way for me. Now that I was in high school, I decided it was time I worked things out for myself.

It wasn't easy.

I took to carrying around a dictionary. The thick paperback book contained translations of English words into Mandarin. When the nuns called on me in class, I flipped through the pages like a lawyer searching for her client's alibi. Even meeting people in the hallways took hard work. I would see a girl who looked cool and decide I wanted to make a friend. I'd walk up, say hi, and try to engage in conversation.

After a halting exchange, I would always end up asking her to point out words in my dictionary so I could read what she wanted to say in Mandarin. The process was painfully slow.

Thankfully, I met a classmate who could relate to what I was going through. Julia had been born in Germany, then come to the US while still little. Like me, she had struggled to learn and speak English, and she appreciated when people were patient with her. She was patient with me and told me not to give up. Julia had a knack for understanding me. Even if I could only come up with a few words, she always seemed to be able to piece together what I wanted to say. With the help of the sentences she assembled for me to repeat, I connected with other friends.

In books, people's lives change in a flash. Reality is rarely like that. It's taken me years to understand that the struggles I went through in high school were essential to making me who I am today. Like coal being crushed into diamond, my personality could be refined only under pressure. Fighting to make friends and get good grades showed me that I could accomplish anything if I put my mind to a task. This built in me the belief that whatever difficulties I face, my mind has the power to overcome them. Many times I've wondered, "Is this my limit? Is this where I fail?" The answer has always been, "No." Sometimes I've needed to learn a new perspective. Sometimes I've needed to reach out for help. But never have I met an obstacle my mind couldn't find a way over, under, around, or through. This life I've made for myself—filled with loving family, interesting work, a successful career, and an indomitable will to excel at every moment—came about, thanks to my belief in the power of my mind.

It is my hope that reading my experiences and the lessons I have learned will help students, young professionals, and anyone else who wrestles with self-doubt to embrace the confidence that will propel them forward. As an immigrant, I am intimately familiar with the feeling of having my life upended, the details spilled out like a jigsaw puzzle. Assembling the pieces of my life has exposed me to patterns of thought and action that I otherwise would never have encountered. The learning process I've been through is one I would recommend to anyone, but I know all too well the frustration that goes along with it. Experience has endowed me with a vital understanding. Culture, upbringing, and education all offer ways to confront trials. When all is said and done, though, your mind is what matters.

Chapter Two

Think About the Positive End

Have you ever been driving down a highway when suddenly you see an obstacle in another lane? Though sense would say you are better off where you are, you subtly steer in the direction of the obstacle. This happens because the eyes lead the mind. To keep from crashing into every piece of debris life offers up, you must be mindful about pursuing your goals. Reflecting positively on the good results you can get from your efforts is essential.

Initially, this will require conscious effort, but once you have trained your mind to focus on a goal, you can trust many day-to-day activities to your subconscious. Many days I have started out from home in my car, thinking about everything I have to do when I get to work, only to find myself pulling into the parking lot with only a vague recollection of how I got there. After years of driving, I know enough about the routes that my subconscious can take care of the details. I have found my subconscious mind capable of handling even complex situations, provided that I fix my end goal firmly before I let my mind guide me.

Sometimes what we work toward isn't what we want or need. We rush around, rarely taking time to think about what is important in our lives. Before you set out in your pursuit, stop, sit down, and ask yourself, "What is my positive end?" Dig down below the surface. If you think, "I want money," ask what that money is for. If you think, "I want to get married," ask what you hope to get from married life. How will marriage be different from the state you're in? Soldiers marching through the desert search the horizon for any sign they're close to their goal. The more discouraged they get, the more likely they are to see mirages and think the end is near. If those mirages are off the beaten track, they could tempt the unwary soldier into danger.

You must be attentive to avoid going off course. Having a purpose will help you skip over thought processes and issues that concern other people's plans. Fears that have held you back, concerns about how you present yourself and what others think about you will fade away. Like weary soldiers finally spotting camp a short way off, the excitement of reaching a goal can tap hidden reserves of energy in you. Your exuberance will make even heavy burdens feel light. I have seen this truth firsthand.

My husband, Bernie, is a triathlete. He works at fitness as his full-time job. Head down and focused on his goal, he pushes himself to break free from physical limitations. The first time Bernie participated in a formal triathlon, he told me afterward that as the swimming portion began, he felt panicky, thinking that he couldn't possibly make it across the water. What got him through was remembering his training. He had felt exhaustion that was worse than what he was about to go through. He had pushed hard and survived, growing stronger after repeated effort. His nervousness was no surprise. He'd set a challenge for himself that most people never dream of taking on. But he knew from experience that he was capable of meeting that challenge. As much as fear made him want to quit, he knew that he had the strength to continue. His mental image of the finish line pushed him to give his all.

I don't run triathlons with Bernie, but I do help with logistics and moral support. I'm also his personal cheerleader. I've seen the change in his face when he hears me screaming his name from the sidelines. A surge of confidence elevates him, making him forget the pain and exhaustion of his sport. When you work with an end goal in mind, you will need people to cheer you on, too. It's up to you to determine precisely what help you need and to communicate this clearly. Think about the difference family and friends can make in your life, the role they can play in your success. Graciously accept whatever aid they have to offer, and don't ever be embarrassed to ask for more.

Every millionaire, philanthropist, and head of state can list a dozen mentors and supporters, not to mention family members, who have been critical in their struggle to get where they are. That's why award ceremonies put time limits on acceptance speeches. If everybody who ever achieved something thanked all the people whose shoulders they stood upon, the ceremonies would never end. When we are children, we refused our parents' helping hands, saying, "I can do it myself!" As adults we realize that our achievements are more impressive when they inspire others to assist in reaching our goals.

Whenever you feel unhappy, take a moment to think about the positive end you want to reach. Are you making progress? Is the goal you're pursuing still right for your life? Whatever matters most to you is what you should chase after. If you don't know what that is right now, take some time to write down what you want to obtain, achieve, or understand. Read what you've written, then sleep on it. Let your subconscious be your guide. When you tune in like this, you'll find knowledge and information that seek you out. Sometimes ideas pop into your head. Sometimes a coworker says what you need to hear without being asked. However it happens, you will find clarity. I don't know where such insight comes from, I'm just thankful for all the help I get.

Coming from an Asian background, family obligations have always been especially important to me. Respect for older family members is a foundation of life in Asian culture. Children are expected to follow strict rules of etiquette when dealing with their elders. Expressing a contradictory opinion is strictly taboo. As a child, I had a terror of confronting my parents. However, after seeing some of the experiences of my peers, I felt I had to let Mom and Dad know where I stood on certain matters. The exact incident we discussed has faded from memory, but I do remember the main point. Mom and Dad wanted to protect me from failure. Personally, I've always believed it's okay to fail. Falling down teaches us to get up. I said as much, and to my surprise, Mom and Dad agreed to support whatever choice it was that had triggered their concern. By expressing myself, I'd given them a chance to share in my decision-making process. They were impressed by my reasoning ability and afterward allowed me more freedom.

A few years ago, I shared that experience of talking to my parents with a mentee, a young woman who had grown up in a traditional Indian household. She was unhappy because her parents wanted her to work in a dental office whereas her big dream was to be a social worker, to make a difference in her local community and around the globe. I impressed on her the necessity of sharing this dream with her parents, despite their differing views. Recently I ran into her. She was glowing with happiness. After our previous discussion, she'd engaged her parents in the conversation she'd been dreading. Though they were skeptical at first, they eventually gave their approval. My friend went on to work with the United Nations, having a positive impact on people's lives in third world countries. Today she is living her dream because she did not let fear of how her parents would react stop her from doing what she knew was right.

Parental support is a huge help for children trying to realize their dreams, but the children themselves are the ones who must set goals, make plans, and act on good advice. The same dynamic exists in the workplace. Managers and executives can be invaluable assets to those who look to them for guidance. Wise leaders scout for talent and do everything they can to encourage development of skills. But there are always more followers than there are leaders. A goal-oriented subordinate must take every opportunity to reach out to supportive leaders, expressing strengths and asking for help in areas he or she has room to grow. Try this for yourself and you will find that leaders, peers, and the unseen patterns of the universe have a way of opening doors.

No one can dream for you, so only you can express the full extent of your dreams. What are your goals for ten years down the line? Now is the time to decide where you want to be and to make plans to get there.

When I was a young girl, I overheard a conversation involving my cousin Roger. For many years he had worked for a company as a programmer. He worked hard and had good technical skills. Yet he was passed over for promotion time and again.

I remember wondering what Roger was lacking. After many years in a leadership position, I now think I know what held him back. Though his work was good, Cousin Roger lacked soft skills—qualities that engage the trust of management and coworkers, making clear a person's competence and approachability. In my experience, people from a similar cultural background to Roger and myself have difficulty understanding the importance of these skills. We are taught that if we keep our nose to the grindstone, promotions will come. In reality, if managers don't see you displaying soft skills, they cannot assess your ability to go beyond your existing tasks. Hard skills demonstrate that you are capable of doing the job you have now; they say little about your advancement potential.

We define professions in terms of hard skills. A woodworker is good at working with wood, a programmer at programming. Soft skills are harder to quantify. They aren't confined to a single vocation. This, in fact, is part of their value. Examples of soft skills include clear communication, as well as the ability to collaborate, to negotiate, to mentor individuals, and to coach a team. You can practice such leadership skills in a variety of settings. These skills will connect you with people at all levels of an organization and help you identify new opportunities for yourself and the company.

Take a moment to think about your career plan. What soft skills will be of most help to you in reaching your next milestone? Look around for people who excel in those skills, both inside your company and in the larger world. Imitate their example and act every day like you are interviewing for your next position. When you learn something new, find a way to engage with others who share your drive and ambition. When you give without expecting anything back, your store of knowledge will compound the interest. The goodwill you put away for a rainy day is also invaluable.

Cultural context and personal histories play in to how we pursue goals. For example, we respond to perceived weaknesses in a project plan in different ways. Hierarchies exist for a reason and should be respected, but there are times when contradicting a superior's opinion is essential. Many successful businesses are built on a culture that expects feedback at all levels. If an executive doesn't have all the facts, how can she make a good decision?

I have personally experienced what can go wrong when members of a team don't speak up about minor problems at an early stage. Little bugs in a system compound over time. Problems that go unresolved can fester, eventually becoming so complex that tracing symptoms back to their cause is all but impossible. If you come from a culture where it is considered unthinkable to draw attention to the mistake of a superior, think about how much embarrassment you can save by speaking up before the molehills have a chance to become mountains. Small, contained problems are easier to talk about than system-wide defects. If your culture says, "Keep quiet!" while your mind says, "Speak up," remember what matters.

At one point in my career, an unexpected change occurred in my life. Circumstances left me without a position. For the first time I found myself out of a job. This could have been discouraging. I admit my circumstances were a surprise. Was I left stunned, unable to act? No, I was not. For many years, I have built relationships with search firms, recruiters, and leaders both inside and outside my industry. I've kept my résumé up to date, adding new skills and accomplishments. Such preparations are not a sign of disloyalty. In a large corporation, every individual is expendable. Savvy department heads respect workers who are ready to land on their feet. If they recognize your value, they will do everything they can to keep you happy where you are.

One easy way to endear yourself to recruiters is by passing on the names of friends and colleagues. I've frequently been contacted about the possibility of moving to a new company at a time when I was happy where I was. After saying as much to the recruiter, I am usually asked, "Do you know anybody who might be looking for an opportunity?" Instead of dismissing this question, I always give it serious thought. On all but a few occasions, I have been able to offer up a name. Of course, I never do this without the permission of the individual. It is amazing how many job seekers I hear about at business and social gatherings now that people know I am willing to help out.

As you set out to pursue your positive end goal, negative thoughts will occasionally try to drag you down. When this happens to me, I read a motivational book or listen to an audio recording I've downloaded in advance. Make sure you always have something like this ready when you need it. That means reading or listening while you're in a good place, not waiting until you're feeling discouraged. Reading self-improvement books should be part of your weekly schedule. Make notes in your career plan about go-to resources for bolstering positivity. Books, magazine articles, and podcasts you find encouraging can serve as lifelines to raise you out of self-doubt.

Setbacks will happen, but they need not be a distraction. If you've reached what appears to be a dead end, ask what good you can get out of the situation. Stepping back to examine the big picture may reveal unexpected advantages to the new path you've been forced to take. The job loss I mentioned earlier put my networking abilities to the test. Thanks to connections I had made, I was able to get back on my feet with barely a break. Through that outcome, I felt validated and motivated to continue sharing my strengths with others.

Being positive is especially important when you're setting an example for a team to follow. As a leader, you must clearly express your vision. Your team members won't always maintain objectivity. Individual agendas can easily pull a project off course. Part of your role as leader is to take a broad view and help others do the same. Connect the dots for your team, showing them the "why" of corporate decisions. "Because I said so!" doesn't work for adults. Your team needs to see how their efforts are affecting the company's future. This goes double when you're working with coworkers on a personal initiative. Simply giving instruction isn't enough. You must show the team your passion and the faith you have in what you're doing together. Give them a purpose and they'll follow you anywhere.

Apply an end-goal perspective to every question you ask your team. Don't burden individuals with emotional demands. When something goes wrong, following this guideline is especially difficult. But questions like, "What were you thinking?" don't provide information you can use. "How can we fix this?" is better. By focusing on the end result, you will be able to ask questions that help your teammates stay positive and be better than great.

My own experience as a mentor emphasizes this fact. Despite all the demands my executive schedule makes on my time and energy, my investment in others has definitely paid off. Many times I have seen the potential in team members and have approached them with advice. These encounters have proven invaluable in pursuing my goal to create an environment of mutual respect and support. I have also benefited from going beyond the team. Helping colleagues step up to the next level in their careers is a great way you can pay favors forward. Be assured that even if you never collect from the individual in question, the universe will find some way to balance the scales.

You'll have caught on by now that my idea of how to run a department doesn't leave room to isolate myself. Whenever I can, I take my laptop to the work floor and pop in on people at their desks. This lets them know it's okay to pop into my office. My door is always open, so long as I'm not in a meeting. I want my team to feel like a family. This may seem strange to someone brought up in a culture that draws hard lines between work and family life, but I have found it to be a powerful motivator. People in a family go the extra mile for one another without being asked. They don't want to do anything to disappoint their nearest and dearest.

Once, in the middle of a major website launch, I received a personal visit from the head of the marketing department. This was a person I did not report to, who would not be held responsible if I or my department failed to work out our difficulties. Another person in that position might have hid in their office, watching for a chance to place blame if the launch was unsuccessful. But this individual stopped in to say, "I have faith in you." That sincere encouragement made all the difference. My gas tank went from "E" to "F," and I was able to drive the project to the end of a bumpy road. In your communication with team members, don't be afraid to add a personal touch. I have made many visits and written many notes praising subordinates over the years. More than once, when it was time for me to leave a company, people have come up to me saying they remembered those notes. They thanked me for caring and listened when I encouraged them to pass on the positivity.

It is often said that life is a journey. What people new to their careers often don't know is that it's okay to take an indirect path, so long as you keep your destination in the forefront of your mind. The earth is a circle, after all, so walking in straight lines is frequently impossible, and almost always more trouble than it's worth. My own career is a testament to the flexibility of one's future. Those who browse my

LinkedIn page will find a listing of just under a dozen hats I've worn since leaving Drexel University in Philadelphia, PA. These are only my most easily quantified official positions. My charity work and mentoring are absent, as is the considerable effort I have put into networking. It hasn't always been easy to maintain my focus.

Chapter Three

Know Your Strengths, Find Your Passion

In the Western world, personal happiness is held up as every individual's ultimate positive end. But what is happiness? Many people pursue wealth, fame, or a romantic interest, thinking that when the desired prize is in their hands, they will be happy. When they reach their goal, however, many times they're disappointed. Money has made them anxious. Recognition has cost them their privacy. The person they loved from afar has proved frustratingly human up close. The time and bridges they've burned to get where they wanted to be have brought them no closer to the happiness they sought. Countless stories like this are the reason I believe that happiness should not be a destination you seek at the end of a journey. It is much better to be happy where you are.

Easier said than done, right? If you are having trouble with your family, or your career has taken a wrong turn, no doubt your happiness has been affected. The optimism you once had about your future now seems misplaced. Is it possible that you've been pursuing the wrong goals all along? Perhaps, but far more likely is that you have only gone slightly off-course. Letting disappointment become your new normal will not point you in the right direction. Negativity will limit your potential and the potential of everyone who depends on you. When life hands leaders lemons, they make lemonade.

I personally safeguard my happiness by telling my mind what I want. I don't let emotions dictate to me. My end goal is not an impulse, it's a positive outcome I've thought carefully about. Goals are essential to my happiness. Absolute control over all aspects of my life is not. Instead of saying, "I need to double my salary in the next five years or my life is over," I look at the possible outcomes of my efforts and decide what I will accept. Realistically, if I don't get everything I want, will it help if I moan and groan? I decided long ago that complaining about every bend in my life's road is pointless. As long as I'm heading toward the positive end, I might as well have fun along the way. Having accepted that disappointments are inevitable, very little is capable of making me unhappy.

Many people are dissatisfied at work because they feel their position does not call on them to do what they do best. If you have ever felt that way, or even if you have not, I strongly advise that you make a list of your strengths. It is amazing the power that writing things down can have! The mental exercise of naming the advantages that are uniquely yours can uncover surprising synergies. Every time I update my own list, I get the feeling that the universe is looking over my shoulder. Opportunities that make use of my strengths come flooding my way. Several times this exercise has motivated me to apply for and take on roles I previously did not know were available.

Strengths are what you do well, but they are also what you love to do. Do you have a special hobby that occupies your spare time? If money were no object, what would you do for free? It is always best to look for new opportunities when you are working, but if you are ever faced with a lull in your career, look back to your list of strengths and ask if your last position was truly where you wanted to be. Could the downturn you've experienced actually be a good thing for your long-term prospects? As mentioned in the last chapter, it's fine to take detours on the way to your destination. But the purpose of a detour is to get around an obstacle. Reviewing your experiences in light of your strengths will sometimes reveal that you need a radical change.

Be generous when assessing your strengths. You may be able to think of a coworker who is better than you in a particular area, but no one is the best at everything. Your combination of skills is unique and therefore valuable. Have you ever heard a beautiful piece of music and thought, "How did she do that?" No doubt the musician had colleagues, fellow students, and teachers who set a high bar. At some point, she, too, was unsure she could measure up. In the end, she rose to the challenge and created something remarkable.

After you have completed your list of strengths, write down what you have accomplished so far in life. Start by setting a target number, your age multiplied by two. Try to list that many accomplishments. This can be difficult because we don't always recognize an accomplishment when we see it. You may find it easier to think of your most recent triumphs and work backward, since one achievement is often built on another. I understand that making lists of this sort can be intimidating, especially if you come from a culture where it's not common for an individual to take credit for their part in a team effort. Please remember that your employers have made an investment in you. It is not prideful to acknowledge the wisdom of their trust.

If you are a student or recent graduate, academic subjects will likely dominate your list of achievements. That's fine, but don't stop there. Have you been involved in charity work or done service to the community? Has a significant amount of your time and energy gone into taking care of family members? The goals you achieved in these endeavors are worth writing down.

Personally, I have learned much from my family that is applicable at work. Our son Eric takes after my husband in his approach to challenges. This has taught me patience, since their way of doing things is different from mine. Our daughter Emily, on the other hand, is a multitasking perfectionist like me. Watching her confront a problem is like looking in a mirror, and I don't always like what I see. "Am I that much of a perfectionist?" I ask, eyes on Emily. Reflecting on her personality has helped me critique my own thinking. Thankfully, she has made me proud by means of her strong, independent spirit.

If you have been working for many years, you have almost certainly done more for your employers, clients, and subordinates than you realize. Managers look to you in times of trouble, their confidence informed by past performance. Team members seek your opinion, knowing your insight can be a difference maker. Volunteer work, outreach, mentoring—you've done it all! Take a head count of your department, asking what impact you've had on each individual's success. Your network of contacts is an achievement in itself. Cultural norms cause some of us to devalue our role in group efforts. Don't fall into this trap. Give yourself permission to own your accomplishments. When you're feeling enthusiastic after a victory, add to your list. When setbacks make you doubt your worth, remind yourself of all you've done. The best is yet to come.

Two lists should now be in front of you. The first tells your strengths. The second, your accomplishments. The two together create a synthesis, a combination of what you are good at and what you are passionate about that has driven each accomplishment thus far. Look for that relationship. When you find it, embrace it. Do your utmost to leverage the strengths that have proven useful to you. Let your passion fuel your strengths and you will surely actuate your full potential.

All the ways you spend your time should align with your strengths and passions. Examine your skill set to find your own unique combination of outstanding abilities. Look for jobs, projects, and tasks that leverage this combo. Involving yourself in activities like these will make your work so much fun, you won't want the day to end. Your success will be unlimited and your peace of mind complete.

Back when I was sweating through my intensive programming classes at Drexel U, I got so used to looking at code that I started seeing it in my sleep. Years later, when I saw The Matrix, I related to the characters who could spot objects in the streams of characters that made up their virtual world. As much as I enjoyed programming, I had reached a saturation point. Overexposure to my essential hard skill threatened my satisfaction with my career choice. Aware that

I needed time away from a screen, I got involved with the Chinese Student Association, a Drexel-based club that gave those of us with an Asian background an opportunity to support each other in academic and business pursuits.

Being from New York City, my alma mater's Philadelphia location seemed quiet and manageable to me, but several of my classmates who had never lived in a major city were overwhelmed. When I first joined the association, our central activity was getting together to drink tea. I quickly saw a ton of opportunity to help meet people's needs. Nobody asked me to take charge, and I didn't stick my nose in where it wasn't wanted. Still, I knew even then that lifting others to a higher level was a great way to elevate yourself, so I plunged in.

Initially, the boost I gave to my fellow students came in the form of a newsletter. Filling its pages were tips I knew would be useful to Asians living in America for the first time. At first, the text was quite basic. Each issue formed part of a handbook on how to get around the city. Included was advice on where students could go for goods and services, shared member biographies, and contact information for those who needed additional help. Later, we added a schedule of Chinese- and Taiwanese-friendly events. This greatly enhanced the newsletter's popularity, to the point that someone was needed to organize member trips to these events. Who do you think got the job?

One of my favorite experiences from that time was helping to arrange a bus trip from Philly to South Williamsport, PA. We went to watch the Taiwanese national team compete in the Little League World Series. This was in the heyday of the baseball program that propelled my birth nation to seventeen championships. Was I a die-hard fan? Not really. But shepherding two busloads of excited twenty-somethings on an eight-hour road trip was my idea of fun. To be honest, I don't remember if Taiwan won or lost that year, but everyone involved had a great time. Other highlights of this period were the annual Chinese New Year celebrations into which the newsletter breathed new life. Attendance was high, the food was amazing, and everybody there felt a sense of community.

When it came time to examine my role in the association, I discovered something about myself. Some friends asked to nominate me as president. I declined. When they asked why, I explained that I preferred working behind the scenes to make things better. Helping people was my motivation, not awards or titles. Taking on a role as president would have meant changing a formula I knew worked well. It would also have added to an already demanding schedule, so in my analysis, it wasn't worth doing. Though I continued to quietly share in the work of organization, I deliberately dodged recognition. This was a good decision that suited my strengths. Plus, it taught me the importance of weighing every role I'm offered. If a prospective venture doesn't move me closer to my end goal, I have found it best to say, "No, thanks."

Refusing an offer can be quite uncomfortable for someone brought up in a culture that considers it rude for a person to say openly what they do and don't want. This can be a crippling disadvantage in the working world. In the culture of my youth, if a host at a dinner party offered you a drink, you were expected to refuse politely, prompting the host to insist. You would then unerringly accept, expressing gratitude for the gracious provision. This cultural exchange had the force of a ceremony, one I saw played out many times. What confusion this might create in the mind of a Western guest, who is used to having the host take her word that she's not thirsty!

Consider the effect this cultural difference can have in a professional setting. An American boss, for example, might ask an Asian employee about his ambitions for the future. If the employee says he is happy where he is, that may stop the boss from offering the employee a promotion.

The employee thinks, "He will ask me again."

Meanwhile, the boss is puzzled. "I thought he'd jump at the chance to advance," he says to himself. Annoyed at having read the employee incorrectly, the boss moves on to another candidate, leaving the employee feeling jilted or overlooked.

The simple truth is that if you wait for a superior to insist you take what you deserve, it probably won't happen. Being vocal about what you want is better. You must express the strengths and passions that differentiate you. When an opportunity comes along that aligns with your goals, express clearly why it is right for you. This includes speaking up about appropriate perks and salary. In my experience, men are stronger in this area than women. As a department head at several different companies, I have had several men come into my office demanding a raise or promotion. Some have had only 20% of the qualifications they needed, but that didn't slow them down. Was this arrogance or a passion to succeed? Every case was different, but

I will say, whenever an opportunity came up, I could always name a few men who wanted to take it.

On the other hand, it is rare when a woman approaches me with an advancement request. I remember specifically going to one female teammate who was the right fit for a position and asking, "Do you want the job?" She worried she wasn't qualified. I explained that I had sought her out because she was a much better candidate than her male competition. She thanked me and went on to perform brilliantly in her new role. If I had not spoken up, I've sometimes wondered how long it would have taken for her to admit her own greatness.

When you are interviewing for a new job, whether inside or outside your present company, let your interviewer see your power. Don't wait for them to ask why you applied. Express what you are there to accomplish with the enthusiasm of a card player holding all aces. Convey your strengths in terms of what you have accomplished. Explain the thought process that convinced you greater triumphs awaited in the new role. Convey the career objective you'll meet by being accepted, and where you mean to go in the long term. No job is an end in itself, any more than a single page is the entire novel. In my school days the English teacher dropped tomes on my desk that struck like thunderclaps. Scientists registered their impact on the Richter scale. Your career is no less epic. When you mention it, let the echoes resound.

To speak seismically, you must know your subject, and that means doing your homework. For example, before you negotiate salary, make sure you gain insight into the pay range available for someone in the position you want. Online resources can give you an idea, but the last thing you want to do is march into a negotiation with inaccurate information. Universities that teach courses relevant to your field keep a pulse on the trends. That's one good reason to include professors and researchers in your network. Before you sit down at the table, check and double-check with them. That way, when you're made an offer, you'll know if the interviewer is being serious or if she's trying to test your knowledge. Knowing what a competitive offer—complete with benefits, bonuses, and future opportunities—looks like is critical.

The ability to do this kind of homework is, again, a strength I have observed more in men than women. In my experience, even when both have an idea of the salary they should be asking for, men are far more prepared to do the asking. It seems like every time I have offered a salary to a male candidate, he has come back to me with a counteroffer, a higher figure he had in mind. This is a good strategy. It shows the interviewer a candidate knows his worth. Once you know what's expected, salary-wise, at a job, why not prepare some figures to toss at the interviewer? An interview should be a conversation, a back-and-forth discussion of ideas. Being too accommodating is as great a mistake as not being accommodating enough. Voice your realistic salary demands. It is not boasting to tell the employer you plan to do a good job for good pay. Some women I have mentored have needed to be reminded of this fact.

If you feel uncomfortable asking for what you're worth, consider that you may be the only qualified candidate the interviewer will have in front of her during the whole hiring process. During the course of the interview, try to find out how many people she is considering. Gauge her excitement as she pages through your *résumé*. When she expresses interest, spare a thought for the competition. Can any other candidate match your talent, your education, your experience? If not, it's okay to ask for a bigger slice of the pie. Salary negotiations take place because different companies have different needs. If you can bring unprecedented success to a company, asking for an unprecedented salary isn't greed; it's right-sizing. Just be sure you can make good on your promises.

The key to success in the salary game is to make victory a win-win. Speak to the value you bring to the company. What do they stand to gain by employing (or promoting) you? Don't pretend to be the second coming of Warren Buffet. Simply explain why the company's investment in you will pay dividends. Show that you believe in their mission and have the skills to achieve their goals. Go into detail. This is important! Nothing turns an interviewer from hot to cold like vague assurances unsubstantiated by past performance. Tell the story of exactly how you'll exceed company expectations, and you'll have a good chance of sealing the deal.

Of course, not every company has the same resources. A company may value what you offer but lack capital to compete with larger entities. Your job is to examine the big picture and make the best choice for your life and career. Keep in mind that salary cuts two ways. If you ask for a high compensation, the company will expect high performance. I have seen individuals brag about what they will do in a new role only to prove unable to deliver. Executives who help build thriving companies do not tolerate this discrepancy for long. Know your strengths, live your passion, but don't invite stress and embarrassment by raising expectations higher than you can satisfy even with experience and time. In ninety-nine cases out of a hundred, the young executives I have helped grow underestimated their maximum potential. They did not clearly see the need to align their work with their strengths and their passions, so they were unable to balance modesty with personal drive.

Over the years I have heard many great ideas that did not go on to benefit their originators. The reasons for this varied, but my observation has been that people who are better able to sell their ideas to senior management succeed more often and are given greater recognition. Considering that perspective is vital when you're making a presentation.

One famous psychology experiment asked subjects to draw a capital letter "E" on their foreheads. Those who were self-focused tended to draw the letter in such a way that if they could have seen it through their own skulls, the orientation would have been left-to-right for easy reading. People who tended to focus on others drew it the other way. This meant that a person standing in front of the other-focused subject could easily have read what they'd written.

Keep other-focus in mind when you sell an idea. You're not selling it to yourself, after all, but to decision makers. Concentrate on what matters to them. If you have doubts about your speaking ability— or even if you don't—a good way to improve is to record yourself practicing, then watch the video back. Look for ways to make your style appealing, to be personable and authoritative, to be clear without being boring. Before you step up to the podium or conference table, check the Myers-Briggs Type Indicator for what it has to say about engaging different personalities in your audience. You will always speak with confidence if you are talking about your strengths and passions, so go in aligned and you'll come out a winner.

Chapter Four

Put Down the Baggage

As we move through life, we pick up and carry negative emotions like sadness, hate, and fear from one experience to another. Lugging this baggage slows us down, yet I have found that in nearly all cases, the stress that causes it is self-imposed. True, we often experience stress in situations we can't control. But the situations are not to blame. To illustrate, consider the skydiver. Many people are deathly afraid of air travel, but these same individuals get a thrill from jumping out of a perfectly good plane. Nothing is different about their situation. They go up in the air thousands of feet, just like those with a fear of flying. But their reaction to this situation is what differs. In day-to-day life, our own reactions determine whether we feel immobilized or energized by a challenge.

When I'm confronted by a stressful situation, something that gets me upset or makes it hard to stay positive, I apply the rule of three. I ask myself, "Am I going to be upset about this in three days? What about three weeks? Three months? Three years?"

Situations that are not going to remain prominent in my mind aren't worth getting upset about. Sure, if I expect an event to still have significance in three years, then sure, I'll give it extra thought. How often do such matters come up? Quite rarely, in my experience. Most emotional bombshells can be defused by looking a few hours into the future, when they will have lost all power to do harm.

This also goes for negative comments people occasionally direct at me, my company, or my team. Will getting mad change the person's opinion for the better? What about the audience for that comment? If someone states an outright lie, I will of course set the record straight. Then, I'll let it go. Holding on to resentment won't improve my relationship with the speaker or anybody else. Why should I let a naysayer clutter up my head with painful memories? The mind is like a supermarket. I stock its shelves with positive feelings and happy thoughts. The most useful ideas go at eye level, where I can see them when I shop. In the real world, food producers pay good money for prime shelf space. I value my mental real estate even more highly, never letting negative thoughts crowd out the positive.

I began to live by the rule of three because of my husband, Bernie. A few days after a fight early in our marriage, we agreed that since neither of us could remember why we'd been fighting, the reason probably wasn't important. Bernie and I are opposites in many ways. Our minds operate so differently, it's amazing we can communicate. The marriage works in part because we don't expect each other to mirror one another's tastes and habits. If we did, my actions and approaches would seem crazy to him, and I'd fret through life, wondering why he constantly set himself up to fail. The reality—that we're both competent, highly successful people who love and support each other—could not so easily shine through.

I am by nature a multitasker. Drop by my office any day of the week, and I'll happily tell you three problems I'm working on. Bernie, in contrast, is a linear thinker. He takes every task one step at a time. Even after all these years, I catch myself thinking, "Does he understand the urgency of what I said?" Usually I stop myself before a question comes out of my mouth. I know that although Bernie's way is different, it works. He's always been there for me, so why should I burden myself fussing over the details?

As it happens, linearity runs in my husband's family. One time, a group of his relatives volunteered to cook a meal using my kitchen. I was grateful for their generosity, until I observed the chaos of their working state. When I cook, I tidy away constantly. Not so my in-laws. They hauled out every pot and pan, every mixing spoon, and every chopping block I owned! Seeing that sent my anxiety through the roof. Did I shout at them, complain to Bernie, or throw his beloved family members out? No. I reminded myself that they were planning to clean up later, then slipped off to a quiet corner until it was time to eat.

Getting upset at my husband or his family won't improve our relationship. It won't get Bernie and me closer to our goal of maintaining a strong marriage. When we are older, we want to be able to look back on the happy times. What could having unrealistic expectations do but cause unhappiness? Instead of getting mad, I would rather give credit to Bernie and others for showing me that there is more than one way to achieve a positive outcome. I prefer to accept people who are different than me as the wonderful individuals they are.

Experiences like cooking with Bernie's family could drive a wedge between me and his family. They could stay on my mind, waiting to be dredged up the next time we had a disagreement. The rule of three will help you avoid storing negativity in your mind and heart. To shed the baggage that's already there, you have to recognize that you were the one who held on to it in the first place. The contents of your baggage—painful memories, hurt feelings, injustices you had to endure—were not your fault. You are under no obligation to carry them with you. Setting them aside can be tough, but don't lose hope. Every new experience offers an opportunity to let your baggage go.

You might be hanging on to a time someone did you wrong, the pain of losing of a love one, or hurtful words a person you respected said. Dwelling on things you can't change will sap your energy. You'll be stuck looking backward, unable to grab present opportunities and future happiness. Instead of blaming others for your feelings, you must own them. You can't change what happened, but you can choose how you react. Be open to moving forward, and your positive attitude will attract positive results.

Think of your heart as a river. Sometimes trash gets stuck on the rocks. Then a new rain comes. It swells the river, hurling torrents past its banks. The accelerated water can flush away debris, helping the river flow swiftly and gracefully. When you pursue positive experiences, you're inviting that rain. Happiness, exhilaration, the satisfaction of a job well done—all these can wash your baggage away. In a vast waterway, even heavily loaded barges can pass. If baggage is clogging up your positive thinking, watch for a way to widen out. Don't be content as a trickling stream. Be the Nile. Be the Mississippi. Burst the dam and be the flood.

Sometimes a *lack* of experience makes up your baggage. This could make you fearful, like you want to run back to your comfort zone. Take my move from Pennsylvania to North Carolina, for example. Even though I was in my forties when I relocated, I was more stressed out about it than when I moved from Taiwan to the United States. In my teens, I didn't know enough about where I was going or what my life would be like to be afraid. As I got older, I learned to play the "what if?" game. All these terrifying scenarios came into my mind. What if my new job doesn't work out? What if we don't get along with our neighbors? What if the kids don't like the school? All these what-ifs were self-imposed. None were necessary.

Years ago, I attended a yearlong course called Leadership Charlotte in Charlotte, North Carolina. Our class—Class 37, best class ever!—wore our enthusiasm on our sleeves. Each month, instructors guided us through a new program for developing our skills. The course kickoff was a particularly difficult physical and emotional challenge for me. Please understand that I am a fit person. Health is important to me. Without health, you can't do anything. Still, there are certain activities I'm more cut out for than others. The rope course that confronted me that first day was my worst nightmare!

For those who have never seen such a course, imagine a giant structure like you'd see at a kids' playground, only giant size. Better yet, picture a pirate ship; now get rid of the bow and sails, leaving only the masts; string ropes to make connections from beam to beam; then imagine pirates dressed in helmets and harnesses, with carabiners attached to safety lines. You've got it! Some people would look at that contraption and think it looked fun. Not me. I have never dealt well with heights. Looking up three stories at the ropes my instructors expected me to scramble across filled me with an almost paralyzing fear.

I didn't think I could make it up to the first stage, much less complete the course. But this was a leadership challenge. I wouldn't be going alone. Everybody in the group depended on everybody else. Class 37 would succeed or fail together. Though I wasn't forced to go, I wasn't going to accept failure without a fight. After much encouragement, I told the instructors, "I will give it a try, but if I freeze, you will have to get me down."

On the first part of the course I was paired with a colleague, sandwiched between other pairs ahead and behind. As I watched, the pair in front mounted boards attached by loops to parallel ropes so the boards could slide along like train cars on a track. Each of the pair pulled themselves along by means of a guide rope, arriving on a stable plank after a minute or so. The partners went in single file so the lead couldn't go back without asking extra work from the tail. After the guides below hauled the boards back by means of trailing lines, I was directed onto the lead plank. My companion waited as I started to pull myself across. I didn't think, "So far so good." I didn't think anything at all. I was too scared to do anything but reach one hand over the other, concentrating my full energy on that simple task.

Midway along the track I remembered how high up I was, and froze. My partner swayed to a halt. The boards shimmied, ready to fling us off. Panic gripped me in its teeth. The rope groaned at the pressure from my fingers. I summoned breath so I could yell at the instructors to get me down, but my teeth were clenched tight. As I willed my jaw to open, my teammates took up a cheer, from ahead, behind, and below.

"Yay, Ivy!" they said. "You can do it!"

I appreciated their sentiment, but to be honest, the confidence they showed in me only made me feel worse. I knew for certain I was going to let them down. Then I heard a woman's voice say, "Look forward. Don't look down. One hand over the other."

This wasn't a voice in my head but a flesh-and-blood colleague who knew how I felt. Her instructions were clear and powerful. I felt my own strength returning. I did as she commanded, pulling myself along very slowly. At long last, I stepped off the board. The platform under my feet was higher than I ever wanted to be, but at least it was stationary. Later, I talked to the lady who had cheered me on. We developed an instant rapport and worked productively together whenever we were paired on projects thereafter.

As productive as that relationship proved to be, the takeaway is that being shoved outside my comfort zone gave me the opportunity to wash away a barrier to growth. The rope course itself showed me that even tasks that seem impossible don't need to stop me. When

I'm confronted by a difficult challenge, I can seek mentors to tell me what to do and teammates to cheer me on. Some people found the course easy, even fun. The fact that it was terrifying to me gave me new insight on the difficulties others may have with tasks I think are easy. I've experienced times when I was less than sympathetic to a team member facing a challenge I felt was within their capabilities. Now, whenever I see a wide-eyed look in the eyes of someone feeling overwhelmed, I recognize it.

It's not enough to give such a team member the usual support. A person who is confronting fear—whether a fear of heights like mine or fear of failure at work—needs extra coaching, extra encouragement, extra feedback. It took all the strength and will I had in me to attempt that rope course. If not for the simple yet effective help of my friend, I would have remained frozen halfway through the first leg. That is why I tell my team members that there is no shame in acknowledging their limitations.

"Ask for help," I tell them. When they do, I give guidance without judgment. I know that the day will come again when I'll need encouragement myself. Helping others exceed themselves is another way to swell the river of your life.

Breaking out of your comfort zone is an essential part of letting your baggage go. As I'm sure my triathlete husband would agree, if you have not pushed yourself to the point of failure, you have not pushed enough. Every time you fall down is a chance to get up. Every "no" you get is one step closer to a "yes".

There have been many major times in my career when I was encouraged to get out of my comfort zone. Some of the jobs I was encouraged to take were intimidating, because I had no prior relevant experience. Fortunately, what I did have were executive sponsors who recognized abilities in me that I did not even know I had. The first time this happened, I walked away from a proven, familiar software development role to take on an entry-level position as a web developer. Understand, this was in 1995, when the Internet was just getting started. Looking back, I can see that this move was the starting point of my successful digital career, but at the time it looked like a huge risk.

The second time was when the business wanted me to take on a newly created information architect role. My initial reaction was, "I have never studied this and know nothing about it. How can I be the best choice?" In retrospect, the position aligns perfectly with one of my core strengths. A similar situation occurred when I was asked to lead the development team who would accelerate QVC.com's online sales to the one-billion-dollar mark. Having been away from technology for six years, I had no idea why the executives in charge thought I could successfully lead a group of top developers. It turned out they were right in their confidence. Under my leadership, the team delivered everything the company asked of me, ahead of schedule.

As I learned, you can't jump the high fence of your fear with baggage weighing you down. Also vital is being on the lookout for opportunities for change. Back in September of 2015, I challenged myself to take a picture that captured the essence of each day. I decided early on I wouldn't take boring pictures, only those I could look back on later with surprise and delight. The pictures would inspire me to live life to the fullest. That meant I had to maximize the use of my time. From September 2015 to September 2016, I tried out new experiences every chance I got. My adventures broke down barriers I hadn't even known were holding me back.

One picture shows me walking a fashion runway. This was not something I wanted to do. Normally I'm quite shy about being the center of attention. But a sponsor of the National Retail Federation Scholarship pledged to donate $10,000 to charity if all the members of a board I was on would take a turn. When I heard the offer, I blurted out, "Yes!" before my brain could say no. I walked to the end of the runway without meeting anybody's eyes. When I reached the spot where I was supposed to turn around, I blinked my eyes and thought, "How did I get here?" My legs went wobbly and I barely had strength to make it back behind the curtain. A colleague snapped a pic for me so that I could prove to doubters, myself included, that I had made it down the runway and back.

An event designed to educate Charlotte's leaders about the municipal justice program gave me another opportunity. Before this event, I had never even held a gun, let alone shot one. With my team, I participated in shooting simulation practice at the police academy. We were instructed on how to make split-second decisions to shoot or not shoot when a target appeared on video. Some of these targets looked like armed attackers. Some were innocent bystanders. They flashed up so suddenly, my fight-or-flight response went into overdrive. I am sorry to say that I shot an unarmed virtual man. However, I left the academy with a picture of my peace-loving self sighting down a rifle at a paper target, and a new appreciation for the difficult work that police do.

One of my favorite pictures shows me meeting Michael Jordan. This was at an event honoring him as businessperson of the year. When I saw the basketball legend, I thought, "That will make a great picture." It's intimidating to go up and introduce yourself to a celebrity, VIP, or guest of honor at a function. Whenever I feel nervous in a situation like this, I remind myself that he or she is a person like me. Being isolated is no fun for anyone, so celebrities are often glad to be approached by somebody with a friendly face and a willingness to talk. In Mr. Jordan's case, the pic-a-day challenge motivated me to walk up and introduce myself. He was quite nice, and so tall compared to me that he had to stoop to get in the picture frame.

Getting the idea? Taking a daily snapshot of my life motivated me to go outside boundaries I'd lived comfortably inside all my life. If you are frustrated with the progress you are making in your career, you owe it to yourself to figure out what's holding you back. Are negative thoughts, memories, and feelings weighing you down like heavy baggage? Is fear holding you back from exploding out of your comfort zone? The solution to both difficulties is the same. Find a mentor. Ask for extraordinary help. Push yourself to burst your boundaries, and soon your baggage will be washed away. Your fears will vanish behind you down the river of your life.

Chapter Five

Where There's a Will, There's a Way

Human beings are amazing creatures. We're not like the computers of today, those excellent calculators that are brilliant at following directions but incapable of doing anything else. We break our own programming all the time, going outside the bounds of prior experience through creativity and imagination. Anytime I have been faced with unexpected obstacles in life, I have found my way by being open to possibilities, allowing my mind the freedom to blaze new trails. Even when I have been afraid of what I had to do, I have been able to let go by stepping back from the situation, seeing it from a fresh perspective, and thinking positively about a solution.

I have experienced the truth of the saying, "Where there's a will, there's a way." That is easy to say. The proof is that I am where I am today. My parents' plan to steer me toward a future as a doctor or an engineer was fine by me. I didn't object to their vision, and my strength in math steered me in the direction of a technology career anyway. However, my struggles with language after we moved to the US made my future uncertain. I was a hardworking student with the ambition to succeed. But would wanting it be enough?

One thing that made mastering the English language hard was the impractical nature of my early learning. The conversational English I'd memorized did little to help me comprehend my literature classes, which challenged even native-born classmates. Comprehension had never previously been a priority of my education. My grades reflected this oversight. Most of my teachers were patient, however, and thanks to the extra time and attention they gave me, I was able to maintain a decent GPA. Still, even in my junior and senior years of high school, effectively processing a single chapter of some of the novels I was required to read took me hours. And sometimes I was supposed to be reading three chapters a night!

I was being asked to do the impossible, fitting in more hours of painstaking study than I could free up on any given night. I could only go without sleep for so long, so I had to find a way to use my time in a smarter way. In thinking about this problem, I was motivated to turn a disadvantage into an advantage. My fellow students, who were better at reading English than I was, relied on CliffsNotes to get through our literature classes. I couldn't do that. The notes were still too long for me to read in their entirety, and I had no way to figure out where the questions I knew we were going to be asked were likely to be answered in the notes. I also couldn't simply skim through the pages of the novel to figure it out. The novel didn't make sense!

Solving this problem was impossible with the tools I'd been given, so I had to think outside the box. Instead of wasting hours staring at the assigned chapters in English and only understanding some of the facts, I shopped around for Mandarin translations. These weren't easy to find in the days before Amazon. Some of the books weren't famous enough to have been translated into my native language. But when I did get my hands on a translated edition, the difference was amazing. I wasn't stuck simply memorizing answers to questions. I actually got to enjoy the books I read and comprehend what my teachers were trying to teach! This practice opened a whole new world to me.

Using the translated editions, I got to know the novels better than my CliffsNotes-reading friends. I knew how the characters spoke to each other. I knew their motivations, not just what they said to each other. If the color of a boat was important in a way the CliffsNotes authors hadn't realized, I was the one who could raise my hand and say what color it was. Questions like that flew over my classmates' heads. Following my will to succeed, I found a way not only to measure up but even to excel.

Out-of-the-box thinking proved essential to my getting good grades, but it was never all I had going for me. Teachers and friends were a huge help. I greatly missed their support when it came time to face one of the greatest challenges of my school career. In order to graduate, all high school students in New York state are required to undergo the dreaded Regents Examination. College-bound students especially must do well, since their scores are considered by collegiate boards. Before all my previous tests, I'd been able to count on receiving advice from teachers who wanted me to succeed. They knew my performance would rise and fall depending on how much work I had to put into bridging the language gap, and generously gave me personalized instruction. I'd have no such help going into the Regents, the contents of which were decided by a state board. There would also be no participation curve, no extra credit to bolster my grade. I had to face the biggest exam of my high school career alone. My future was at stake.

Everyone eventually faces a crisis of this sort. We all have support structures we get used to relying on but must eventually do without. At work, I have found myself having to pick up the slack from an absent team member. In my executive leadership roles, I have weathered upheavals due to corporate reorganization or my own circumstances. And like every parent before me, I vividly remember being left holding my new baby after the relatives went home. Coping in such a situation is 10% perspiration, 90% preparation. Only by acknowledging your weaknesses and leveraging your strengths can you prevail.

I put my mind to the problem of the Regents Exam. I asked myself, "How can I apply the methods that got me through school?" I researched how the test was given. Every year, thousands of hopeful seniors sit through the hours-long exams. Answers are mostly multiple choice. As a math whiz, I knew the odds of filling in the right bubbles at random were against me. I needed a solid grasp of the material to secure my future. Or, I came to realize, I needed a good understanding of the test itself. Not all the old tests are thrown out after students sit for them. Bookstores keep archives of exams from prior years for concerned students like myself to buy.

The old tests I purchased quickly revealed some interesting patterns. For one thing, the questions weren't all new every year. How could they be? There are only so many ways you can ask which US president approved the Louisiana Purchase. Sets of questions were cycled in and out. Sometimes, questions were asked in a different order. Answer A might change places with answer C. Only rarely did the text of a question or its right answer change. Armed with this knowledge, I sought help from my teachers and friends. We studied topics I knew I was weakest in. After several weeks, I still had trouble comprehending certain subjects, so I fell back on my gone-but-not-forgotten habit of memorization. By the time I sat the Regents, I knew the old tests so well that if a recycled question came up anywhere, I was sure I could recognize it and choose the right response.

It's funny that the learning method I had moved to the US to get away from was what closed the gap for me in the end. This experience showed me the value of having a variety of crowbars in my mental toolkit. I have never been afraid of hard work. The expression "work smart, not hard" sets up a false dichotomy, in my opinion. Those who work hard at working smart and always stay on the lookout for better ways to work make the most of their opportunities. When my grades for Regents came out, I saw that my strategy had proven true. I was even a little shocked to see how highly I had placed. Will had found a way.

My scores opened the door to any university education I wished to pursue. I applied to several prestigious schools, all with excellent technology programs. The first letter I got back was from the most prestigious on my list—a rejection. I was disappointed, but by that time, I had learned to take bad news in stride. Little pebbles on the road of life weren't going to make me stumble. I was born to scale mountains. Friends and teachers took the rejection worse than I did, but even their frustration didn't last long. Out of nearly a half-dozen schools, only my first respondent turned me down. All my other choices said they'd be happy to have me. I was left to decide which one suited my goals.

I chose Drexel largely because they offered a co-op program that was quite attractive to me. As a participant, I would spend half of my sophomore, junior, and senior years as a full-time student and half interning for a partner employer while taking a reduced class load. The work experience would be a great head start toward reaching my career goals. The only catch was that the co-op schedule was expected to keep me in university for a full five years. Conquering the Regents had made me so confident that I challenged Mom and Dad to a wager of sorts. I told them I was sure I could finish my curriculum in the standard four years instead of five, without neglecting my internship. They agreed that if I kept my grades up through this period, they would donate the remainder of the tuition money they'd set aside to the Ivy Independent Living Fund, aka my bank account. Eyes on the prize, I set out to conquer the world.

Soon after that, my optimism took a hit. To be fair, the goals I set for myself were often unreasonable, so I should not have been surprised when the inevitable happened and I failed to reach one. But I was. One day I came home from class depressed, having received a less-than-perfect test grade. I felt horrible, like my whole future was ruined. The funny part, in hindsight, is that even though my numeric score wasn't as high as I wanted, my letter grade was still an A. After finding out what had upset me, my roommate put things in perspective.

"Ivy," she said, "who cares if you didn't get 100%? An A is an A!"

Honestly, I had never thought about things this way. In my mind, perfection was the goal, and anything less was unacceptable. But I saw immediately where she was coming from. The few points I'd shed weren't enough to be acknowledged by a change in letter grade. They wouldn't even hurt my GPA. So, what was I worried about? My expectations were only in my head. Nobody else would judge me as harshly as I was judging myself. If my roommate had walked in with the same grade, I would have told her, "You go, girl!"

I will justify including this anecdote in a chapter about willpower by saying this: If you set goals conducive to your strengths and summon the will to work for them, your mind has the power to succeed. Dispute this truth all you want to, but you'll live better believing it. No one passes every milestone unchallenged, but if you are struggling with frequent defeats, might it be the way you measure victory that is out of balance? Instead of demanding perfection from yourself, commit to thinking positively while acting in pursuit of your end goal. In all areas of your life, keep your expectations thoughtful, reasonable, and realistic. By applying appropriate standards to your performance, you will be able to accurately gauge advancement. By applying them to others, you will alleviate interpersonal pressure, maintain open communication, and keep a sharp eye out for ways you can help them progress.

Changing your perspective on what is acceptable is not always easy. Years of ingrained habit, encouraged by Mom and Dad's high expectations and my A-plus-obsessed culture, made it hard for me to stay positive. As a team leader, I have often encountered standards different than my own. At times, I've been baffled by poor performance from my team members. I have found consistently that getting upset hurts more than it helps. When deadlines are looming, I don't chastise my team for slowness. Instead, I assure them of my continued faith. I trust our preparations and our collective will. I know that if the worst does happen, we'll have time after the disaster to assess.

Stress is a burden in such circumstances, but it can be overcome. When the pressure's on, I use a simple trick to stop the negativity train in its tracks. Wherever I'm likely to be negative, I make sure to put something in front of me that can take my mind in a positive direction. When I worked for shopertainment retailer QVC, I used to go for walks through our studios, distracting myself for a short time by watching whatever live show was going on. As a senior vice president at Belk, I kept a collection of designer chocolates in my office. Very therapeutic! I've heard of offices that let people bring in dogs or cats, which can be comforting. A furry pet can offer considerable stress relief in offices that will accommodate one. Think carefully about what will help you cope with stress.

Taking care of yourself is never a waste of time. Even industrial robots need down time and maintenance checks. You are far more than a machine. Your mind is the engine that drives everything you set it to do. Plan ahead to nurture your mind and body so stress will not get in the way of your goals. Remember that you and your team members are human. Set reasonable goals, pursue them with purpose, and they'll support you. The best way to lead is by example. When you are faced with a difficult, draining task, sometimes all you can do is let yourself be drained—of energy, that is, not conviction. Believe in yourself, respect your team, and trust your will to work out a way.

Chapter Six

Priority Is Productivity

The internship opportunity that began my sophomore year brought me to Merck & Co., an internationally known pharmaceutical developer and manufacturer. I loved my time at Merck, and the corporate culture changed my outlook. My role was supporting IT products for people on every tier of the organizational chart, so I got to meet several company higher-ups outside my direct superiors. Many were eager to share their hard-won wisdom, and all appreciated that I was willing to learn. One topic came up repeatedly in conversation with these executives. The key to productivity, they said, is setting the right priorities.

That was not a lesson I thought I needed at the time. I had survived a trans-Pacific, cross-country move, plus immersion in a new language by tackling everything, all the time. Multitasking and out-of-the-box thinking was all I had ever needed, aside from the gracious help of teachers and friends. Whatever the challenge, I had never felt the need to portion out my time and effort. When the going got tough, I put in more time, more effort.

In the real world, maximum effort does not always equal maximum results. Employers expect our full-time attention. If we have time or energy to spare, there is always more work to do. All work is not created equal, however. Getting bogged down in "busy work"—work that is created to give somebody something to do—can detract from both the quantity and quality of effort you put into important tasks. At Merck, I was invited to receive training in a time-management system that is extremely effective at separating trash projects from treasure. I've found it to be incredibly powerful, yet it is so simple I can sum it up in three letters: ABC. My mentors swore by this method. Every piece of paper that crossed their desks went into one of three slots labeled with these letters.

Papers in the A slot are do-or-die missions. If these high-stakes tasks aren't completed, business processes slow down, growth stagnates, and everyone in the company suffers. A-tasks must be given the most fervent attention. They call for the most stringent accountability. If an overworked executive can only finish one task a day, it must be an A-task.

B-tasks are one step down. They are projects somebody wants to get done, but if they do not, business as usual will continue. Many pet projects belong in the "B" category, as they are often inspired by new and emerging technologies that can help a business grow. The health of a corporation, the executives explained, can be measured by how much time people find to focus on B-tasks.

Tasks in the "C" slot are not throwaways, but they usually do not impact business day-to-day. They are the optional upgrades that enhance efficiency or add future-proofing to processes that already work well. If a C-task is deleted from somebody's to-do list, its loss doesn't impact that day's production, or the next day's, or the next's. C-tasks are bonuses. If people get around to them, great! When the pressure's on, they don't get looked at.

Learning this simple ABC system changed my life. When I first started my internship at Merck, I thought I was ready to write the book on productivity. Soon I learned that if I didn't have the right priorities, it didn't matter how hard I worked. Like a sprinter getting ready to run a marathon, I needed to pace myself. Wearing myself out would do no one any good. Worse, if I put energy into running the wrong way, I could make things harder for myself and others. Expending all my energy on low-priority tasks would be similarly destructive.

Years after taking this all in, I was promoted to a VP position at QVC.com. In my first few weeks, I was stunned by the volume of my executive workload. It was hard to imagine how anyone could shoulder so many responsibilities. Often I felt like I was drowning. To control my panic, I asked some experienced colleagues how they managed to do it all. One person gave me an answer that has proved essential to my success. She said that none of the executives who impressed me so much were truly as on top of things as they appeared. They used prioritization to handle the most important tasks themselves and delegated the rest.[1] When you're operating at an executive level, there's

---

1 This same wise colleague was the source of another piece of advice. In addition to prioritizing their tasks, she said, executives handle their workloads by "managing perception." This was a new concept to me at the time. Years of experience have deepened my understanding of its importance, so I will be devoting a fair bit of chapter eight to sharing my thoughts on the subject.

not enough time to clear your calendar. Only by setting priorities can you personally tackle your A-tasks and maybe one or two Bs. Everything else had to be passed to people you could trust.

After hearing this revelation, I took a bit of time to reflect. When I had moved into my new position, I had planned to face the challenges by raising my game. But the rules of the game were totally different from what I'd thought they were. To win, I had to reinvent myself. I had to reassess the values I'd been used to acting on. No longer would demonstrating the traits that had gotten me promoted be enough. Some of those very traits could cause me to fail.

At my friend's suggestion, I tried an exercise where I wrote down my "buckets"—the projects, daily tasks, and distractions I was spending time on. I included the percentage of time I thought each bucket should take per day. Then I went back through my calendar, tracking my past three months of activity. I compared the actual percentage of time each bucket was taking with my estimates and had a shock. My buckets were upside down! The tasks with the lowest priority, that I had intended to give the least time, were consuming the most. My important projects were starving because I fed them leftover minutes, nothing like the hours they deserved.

Thanks to this reevaluation, I was able to turn things around. I moved unnecessary meetings and other time-sinks to their proper places and made learning to delegate my first concern. Once I had mastered delegation to a reasonable degree, I set up a daily appointment with myself to go over and adjust my priorities for the day, week, month, and year. In a short time, I became a more effective contributor to the success of my department and that of the company as a whole.

People often ask my advice on gaining a work-life balance. My answer strikes them as surprising. I don't believe any such balance is possible. Instead, I care for my responsibilities through work-life integration. This is not only a semantic difference. It requires that I set career goals that make work rejuvenating instead of draining. Giving to others is a huge part of that. When I see mentees achieve greatness, I feel refreshed. When someone sends me a "thank you" email, I smile. Positive experiences like these energize me to such an extent that I don't feel the need to separate work from leisure. I can enjoy multitasking my goals.

Take, for instance, my husband's triathlon meets. Bernie puts his all into his training, so the least I can do is cheer him on. The events take hours, so I must be smart about how I use my time between laps. If the weather is nice, I may sit in the stands, reading my team's latest site enhancement proposal on my laptop. When it's muggy or cold or rainy, I shelter in my car or back at the hotel. I know approximately when Bernie will swim or cycle or run past the stands, so I'm able to go over paperwork, draft amendments, and make business calls until my alarm alerts me it's time to head back to the venue. I get a surprising amount of work done this way, and my husband appreciates the support.

I take a slightly different approach with the kids. Though I make sure to attend their school events and performances, I don't load up on extra obligations. If you see a mom walking into the auditorium with a half-dozen trays of homemade cookies, that's probably not me. But I will be in my seat, phone on silent, when the principal opens the program. It's a pleasure to support them and let them know how proud I am of their achievements. I grew up in a culture where parents were supposed to be authority figures, not playmates. That makes it hard for me to chat with my kids like the moms you see on TV. But they do know I will be always there for them when they need me.

Early on, getting home in time to have dinner with the children and Bernie was a challenge. I made hitting that deadline a priority and adapted as necessary. Soon we fell into a routine. After reading a bedtime story, I would spend some time on the home computer, finishing up work. During Emily and Eric's preteen years, I decided they should not have to see me working while they were awake. In this way I made it clear that they were my priority. Now that they're teenagers with more stamina than I can muster, keeping up with my schedule is a bigger challenge than ever. I tackle it with consistency and continue to have success.

Thankfully, the people I work with respect my commitment to parenting. They know not to call at certain times and not to expect an immediate response to every text. Though my family has had to make sacrifices over the years, I always assure the kids that even if I have to work while they're around, they can always come to me and say, "Mom, this is important." I will then give full attention to their problems. Because they feel confident that they are the most important part of my life, they rarely make difficult demands.

Time is like a river that flows in only one direction. You can't recycle time you've wasted, just as a plant growing on the shoreline can't soak up water that's already swept by. It is essential to think carefully about how you spend time. Would you throw twenty dollars away for no good reason? Yet many people waste seconds, minutes, and hours that can easily be converted to dollar figures as a fraction of their earning power. Looking back, you don't want to regret wasting time that you could have used to make a difference in the world. Managing time is a challenge for people at all levels of responsibility and every stage of life. To reach your full potential, you must apply your mind to the problem of how to best use your time. Please note that we all have a human impulse to shut others out when we feel pressed for time. This is the opposite of what we must do to have success, advancement, and excellence as a leader. Give to others, and they will give back more to you. Your team members are streams that feed your river. Where many streams meet, the river is powerful.

As you seek to maximize your use of time, avoiding anything that creates friction in your scheduling is essential. Sometimes a cultural component is present in this aspect of your professional life. When an American employer sets a deadline, for instance, what does this mean to you? I have worked with people whose honest, culturally informed understanding is that a deadline is the date when work is to be started, rather than the last possible date it can be turned in. It is easy to see how this could create tension with a boss who expects to see regular reports on progress! Take time to compare your understanding of how to schedule major deliverables with that of the company. Exceeding their expectations is an excellent way to build confidence in your abilities.

Another thief of your time that you must avoid is clutter. The digital revolution has not solved the problem of messy desks, only moved it online. Many of my peers suffer under the delusion that the best way to deal with a flood of emails is to put off dealing with unimportant messages until later. The problem is that later never comes. When I receive a new email, I don't let it sit in my inbox. I reply, delete, or save it to one of several folders I have earmarked for specific follow-up actions. Years of fielding questions from upstream and down have taught me that if I let my inbox fill up, I'll waste time rereading messages in a cycle of concern, excuse, and dismissal.

Concern: Was there something important this email was asking me to do?

Excuse: It couldn't have been too serious, or I would have handled it by now.

Dismissal: I'll take care of it tomorrow.

The importance of a single email takes only seconds to assess, but if you repeat those seconds for ten . . . fifty . . . one hundred emails multiple times a day, they quickly add up. Trim your inbox like you would a garden, preserving flowers and discarding weeds. Don't leave any message the way you found it. Reply, delete, or save for later action. Personally, I have taken this concept further by creating filtering rules for my email software. My folders are color-coded by subject line, sender, and whether I was the only recipient or part of a group list. At a glance I can tell the importance of a message, allowing me to set its priority. Over the years, I have advised many friends and employees on how to keep a tidy inbox. Several have reported to me that this has added precious minutes to their day. Their priorities stayed straighter and they avoided the concern-excuse-denial cycle. The dividend for their up-front investment was extra time and peace of mind.

Chapter Seven

Balance Traditions, Conditions, and Faith

So often we behave in a certain manner because, "It's always been that way." The expectations of the environment we were raised in shaped our thinking. Sometimes, those old ways no longer work, yet we continue to do what they tell us, never asking if they are right. In my case, the ancient traditions that guided my family for generations played a major part in reaching my full potential, but so did the rebellious attitude of Madonna, the queen of pop. Thanks to different points of view I was exposed to in my teen years, I learned that questioning tradition is far more beneficial than blindly accepting its guidance.

Watching the nuns at my school was always educational, even when we weren't in class. These were women driven to follow age-old traditions, something I knew a little about. Though I respected the nuns and appreciated their kindness, I admit there was something fascinating about watching other girls push their buttons. I remember one student who had a hairdo that made a mockery of school rules. On one side of her head, the hair was cut short. On the other, it hung down to her shoulder from front to back, including her bangs. This meant that she walked around all day with one eye covered up. I don't know what you call that look. Punk rock pirate?

I enjoyed watching the nuns look at her and hearing the excuses they made to approach her from the blind side. They wanted so badly to tell her to cut off her hair, but technically, the long and short hairstyles she wore were both allowed. Nobody had thought to write a rule that said the two styles couldn't be combined on one head. The girl's creative expression had a special teenage quality that appealed to me. The school could make us wear uniforms, load us down with homework, and tell us how to spend most of our days, but there were cracks in its authority. All it took to wriggle out was imagination, that same out-of-the-box thinking that helped me survive literature classes. I took this lesson to heart.

Later, I was thrilled to discover the embodiment of creative rebellion in the singer Madonna. OMG, she was so amazing. That hair! That eye shadow! Those bracelets! To my adolescent eyes, she was the Queen of Creative Expression, the Holy Mother of Cool. In school, I copied her style as much as I could get away with. I remember one time I was wearing these crazy big hoop earrings. They weren't circular, more like ovals. It looked like they had started out round, then somebody had stretched them out.

The principal happened to see them as she passed me on her way to the office. She stopped walking and said, "Hey, what happened? Did somebody pull on your earring?"

I knew what she was doing. My look didn't cross any lines, but it pushed against a few. Though we normally got along, the challenge in her eyes demanded I answer back.

So I said, "Like this?" and yanked off the earring.

As I held it out, the principal started back, clutching her chest. She must have expected to see blood streaming down my neck, gory flesh swinging from the bangle. It took her for a moment to register the clip at the top of the earring. At the time, I didn't have pierced ears!

To be honest, I couldn't bring myself to feel bad about giving the lady a scare. Her reaction was too interesting. The intensity of emotion my act had provoked astounded me. All my life I had been taught the traditions of my parents, my culture, and Mom's religion. Tradition was a powerful force in my life. But power cuts two ways. People who follow tradition are confident about their place in the world, yet this very confidence leaves them vulnerable to the actions of people who defy convention. Even minor revolutions can have major impacts on the orthodox.

Sympathetic though I am to other parents, my adoration of the Material Girl convinced me that a little rebellion can be a good thing. Children from Asian cultures are often obsessively protective of their family reputation. It is drilled into us from an early age that everything we do is under scrutiny. This puts a lot of stress on the parent-child relationship. I have always appreciated the work ethic emphasized by my culture. However, the competitive spirit of Chinese parents is something I long ago rejected.

Mom had a good friend in the Asian community, a woman I called Aunty Irene[12]. She stood out to many people, including myself, because of her approach to parenting. Some people gave her grief because she did not conform to Chinese tradition when it came to raising her boys. She let her kids do their own thing more than most in the community. She even let her boys play in a rock band! That was unheard of in a culture where parents bragged about their children being number one in school subjects. Their little go-getters didn't have time to waste on frivolous music.

Aunty Irene saw things differently. She knew her boys had good hearts, so she supported their decisions. To the surprise of many people in the community, her flexibility paid off. When I think about the kids I knew growing up, Aunty Irene's sons became the most amazing examples of success. They achieved much academically, in business, and in life. By letting her boys express themselves, she allowed them to get rebellion out of their systems. After that, they were content to pursue more responsible ambitions.

A contrast is my uncle Peter. His daughter, a girl five or ten years older than me, had a lifelong dream of breaking out as a singing star. Uncle Peter couldn't see any good coming from that life. He put pressure on his daughter, forcing her onto a career path she didn't want at the time. She was successful, eventually graduating from Yale Law. Before she graduated, she was scouted for a position at

2 In the Asian culture, nearly every relationship is defined by a title used with their name. There's not an exact English parallel that means "respected unrelated older woman," so I have used the convention of calling them aunts and uncles. The cousins in this book are really mine, though!

one of the top New York City law firms. Everything seemed to be going great until, after a couple of years, she quit. Her teenage dream still loomed large in her imagination. Leaving everything behind, she took to the road, determined to make it come true. For years she struggled. Her relationship with her father became so strained that they stopped speaking and never started again, even when he became ill near the end of his life.

If Uncle Peter had been supportive early on, I believe his daughter might have found success. More likely, she'd have been able to move on from failure before leaving home. She could have worked through her young dreams, like Auntie Irene's boys, and had plenty of time to pursue a more suitable ambition. At the very least, she and Uncle Peter could have stayed in touch. Life is too long a journey to get mired in one path. Sometimes kids have to follow their hearts before they can follow their heads.

Some diversions along a chosen career path lead to positive outcomes. Others simply waste time. It's not always possible to know the end from the beginning. That's why it is essential to seek good guidance. Personally, I have sought and found excellent advice from several traditional and nontraditional sources. In my opinion, the wisest course is to consider each new piece of wisdom in the context of your life conditions, weighing it rationally and acting in full recognition that you will be held accountable. That being said, I don't reject the idea that forces beyond our conscious understanding have a bearing on what we do with our lives. In fact, the experience I had with the hoop earrings and rock 'n roll convinced me seeking wisdom is not only possible, but a fundamental truth of the universe.

When I was a teenager, safety laws weren't as big a deal as they are today. You didn't see ads on TV or hear warnings on the radio about wearing your seat belt. So guess what? We didn't do it. I didn't even think about buckling my seat belt for most of my young life. Then, one day, I caught a ride home with a group of my classmates. As usual, none of us wore our seat belts. We bobbed and weaved in our seats as the driver wheeled around corners, laughing at whatever piece of gossip we were gabbing about. While we were cruising on a straightaway, I felt a pain in my head. It came on sharply and suddenly. With it, I heard a voice in my head.

"Put the seat belt on," the voice said. When I didn't obey immediately, it repeated, "Put the seat belt on."

I didn't know what to think. Nothing like this had ever happened to me before. The voice was urgent, and obviously associated with the pain in my head. I hoped that if I did what it said, the pain would go away. Wincing, I drew the seat belt across my lap. No sooner had I heard the buckle click than a truck came out of nowhere. My friend's car ricocheted off its fender and struck a tree. I blacked out for a moment. When I came to, I found that my friends were bruised and battered but had come through without serious injury. I was fine too, but judging from the angle of our impact, I could see that if I hadn't been wearing my seat belt, I would have been thrown through the windshield.

I'm not saying the voice belonged to my voice belonged to my guardian angel or that it was a message from God. Maybe it was my own subconscious responding to perceptions I hadn't had time to register in my conscious mind. I can't explain what happened, but ever since that day, I have felt that there is a reason I am alive. Knowing my life has a purpose, even one I don't fully understand, influences the choices I make in many ways. Reflecting back, I can boil these down to two major categories.

First, having a purpose helps me to accept the life I have and the conditions I must live with. Many people feel trapped by situations they can't change. I don't feel the same way. Negative events in my life are challenges I know I can get through. I'm not always happy when I face the unexpected, but I don't feel defeated because I have to struggle for a short time. I look for the good that comes from surviving, the refinement of my skills, the strength fighting back builds. Experience has shown me that I have more control over outcomes than I appear to at first glance. By having a positive attitude and following trustworthy guides, I have been able to benefit from situations that seemed purely negative. Even when I was stuck in circumstances I couldn't change, I've experienced side effects that worked out for the greater good. Accepting my life and environment is a great source of personal peace.

The second way my purpose motivates me is that it gives me a reason to get out of my comfort zone. I've already spoken about how beneficial this can be. Confronting lifelong fears, like my fear of heights, is always unpleasant. Still, opportunities to learn new things excite me. They offer a chance to figure out why I'm here, what I've been preserved alive to do. Whenever I'm in a new place or I'm asked to do something that makes me afraid or embarrassed, I ask myself, "Ivy, could this be part of your purpose?" I can't rule anything out! Many times, curiosity has helped me push through fear, embarrassment, sadness, and anger, as well as every other limiting emotion.

I realize that this spiritual side of my personality may be difficult to understand. Some find it hard to believe in anything they can't see with their eyes. Before the car crash, I felt the same way. Mom had been a Catholic my whole life, but I had always considered myself a skeptic, taking scientific views. Since faith was invisible, I dismissed it as incomprehensible. Yet I couldn't see the voice, and listening to it saved my life.

To any who feel uncomfortable talking about faith, I ask you to please examine the results. Faith in my purpose has made me a happier and more driven person. Everything I have achieved in life has been motivated and assisted by my faith. Faith helped me excel at school. It has guided how I care for my family. Faith has elevated my performance at work. My approach to leadership is both grounded in experience and guided by faith. In every aspect of my life, I have benefited by the peace and motivation faith inspires. Should I dismiss the advice of this competent guide?

In the years since that fateful car ride, I have heard the voice on multiple occasions. Once, while wading into a lake, it warned me not to go deeper. Later, a strong feeling similar to the voice helped me meet my husband. This happened while I was working as a system developer for CertainTeed, a well-known building materials manufacturer. I was attending the annual blood drive. Passing by a table, I made eye contact with a woman I had not seen before. My instinct was to keep walking, but a strong conviction told me that if I stopped and talked to her, my life would change for the better. The feeling was unmistakable, and I had learned by then to trust such impulses. I stopped, chatted, and quickly struck up a friendship.

My new friend introduced me to a nice couple who insisted I meet this guy they knew named Bernie. We were both goal-oriented. We both worked in technology fields. We both played tennis. With so much in common, how could we not hit it off? I find it hilarious to think back on my friends' confidence in the match, because despite our undeniable similarities, if I had read a Myers-Briggs write-up of Bernie's personality type, I never would have given him the time of day. As it happened, our differences have turned out to mean little. At the time of writing this book, Bernie and I have been married more than twenty-five years.

Am I saying that every major decision in your life can or should be made by some subconscious process or a supernatural outside force? Of course not. I believe, first and foremost, in the power of the mind. We are all responsible for our choices, so we need to think each one through. The point of balance I propose is that there are depths reason alone can't fathom. There are perceptions, maybe even forces, of which we are not consciously aware. Consider an analogy from computer science.

In my field, there is no such thing as a truly random number. Bits of code known as random number generators, or RNGs, make use of knowable-but-unknown quantities to simulate random events. An RNG might depend on a program's execution time, or some fraction of a computer chip's temperature to power its computations. Numbers calculated in this way are not truly random, just unpredictable from the standpoint of the programmer. Sources exist for extracting randomness from atmospheric conditions or radioactive decay, but even these values are understood to be pseudorandom. They appear random because we lack the technology to fully understand the patterns underlying their behavior. Nevertheless, the patterns are there.

When we choose to be guided by faith, we are acknowledging that some of the patterns in our lives are beyond our understanding. They are so complex or subtle or both that perceiving them through ordinary means is impossible. Yet they exist. When they are brought to our attention, we are startled, like the principal to whom I handed my earring. Our expectations have been confounded. The universe or something in it has fooled us. Our minds have enough untapped power that we recognize we've received a message, even when we don't know where it has come from. If we keep ourselves open to guidance, we can benefit in ways we have not yet imagined.

Chapter Eight

Manage Perception and Your Brand

Some of the best advice I ever received came from an old boss of mine, Tom. After he lost a previous job, he explained that he realized it is not who you know, but who knows you that counts. Up until we had that conversation, I hadn't been investing a lot of time on networking. My boss impressed on me how critical it is to make connections along the way. Initially, I decided to spend an hour each week on network building. I polished my LinkedIn profile and made sure all the top placement firms were up to date with my achievements. Quite soon, I exhausted the possibilities of this narrow focus and decided to broaden my outreach.

Prior to starting this effort, I'd been doing volunteer work with area schools. Though I had initially been driven by a need to give back, I soon discovered that the events I was participating in put me in touch with valuable contacts from outside my industry. I made some amazing connections with leaders from a variety of fields. My approach was never confrontational. I didn't stick my business card in anybody's face. What I did do was think about what I could do to help others, including the people I wanted to reach. Giving my time and energy without worrying what I'd get back helped me build a reputation as someone people could turn to. As soon as this happened, people from different walks of life reached out to me with advice and opportunities. It's fascinating the lives you can touch through friends of friends, and so reassuring to have people you can rely on in difficult times.

During my tenure at Belk, I was asked to chair a company-sponsored group called the Women's Leadership Network (WLN). The leadership experience I'd gained by planning events for the Chinese Student Association helped make this a success. When I took on the responsibility, the WLN was a small group of employees executing functions back-to-back. Organization was insufficient to scale, so members were seeing limited results even though they were giving their all. I set a goal to change that, first by recruiting many new, capable members, then by pioneering a new infrastructure.

Eventually, we emerged as an organization divided into eight committees that could each focus on a different interest. Committees scheduled events on a staggered schedule so there was always enough time to plan. No single committee, and certainly no individual, had to carry an unreasonable burden. With time on our side, managing events became a bonus for employees. They gained opportunities to develop their skills and show their progress to fellow network members and guests. The quality of our events was excellent, and attendance was high. Thanks to the hard work of all involved, the WLN improved its already good reputation and made a robust contribution to the success of Belk. To this day, the network still operates according to the committee structure I helped architect.

This well illustrates the vital role executives play in a successful company. As an IT professional, bashing out code is part of my job, but if I were to print out every line I ever wrote, the stack of pages would look nothing compared to the combined output of every person I have supervised. The fact is, rarely does an individual's impact on the company exceed that of the team. As a team leader, therefore, I can be most productive by prioritizing the supporting role I play. Just like every ship needs a captain, my team needs me to steer it in a manner that optimizes the use of company time. I can accomplish much more by leading than by attempting to solve problems myself. This is true regardless of my (hard) technical skill.

Back when I was struggling in my first executive role, I said to myself, "Don't worry, Ivy. You can do this. You just need to work a little harder." I hadn't anticipated the demands on my time that leadership would bring. The helpful colleague who explained that I'd have to live or die by my schedule also told me to manage perception of my personal brand.

Perception is how we see or hear or otherwise sense the world around us. To understand my friend's statement, we have to look at how perception functions in a corporate setting. Consider the CEO. From the top of the accountability ladder, how clearly will a chief executive be able to see any given subordinate? That one person is obscured by countless layers of administrative, logistical, and legal concerns. Metaphorically, the CEO's responsibility is the health of the forest. He or she doesn't have time to focus on every tree. Subordinates and lower-level managers must be able to operate without detailed attention from their senior leaders. But if supervisors are not observing subordinates, how can ambitious workers demonstrate their qualifications for advancement?

The answer is personal brand. Recently, while sitting across a meeting table with some junior execs, I was reminded of how hard it used to be to think of myself as having a brand. Only recently have I come to appreciate that personal brand is the only means employees have to sell their individual parts of the company story. Everything else we do gets absorbed into something bigger. Projects are done by teams. Initiatives are completed by departments. Companies have profitable quarters, not you or me or Jenny from accounting. As individuals, we work hard to do our part in the great endeavor. But if we do not also highlight our contribution—if we do not manage perception of our personal brand—we can find ourselves left out of a job when our department or the company undergoes a reorganization.

This is another area where cultural habits can stand in the way of your success. Group achievements are given such importance in some cultures that accepting praise as an individual is looked down on. The expectation is that the person who is praised will apologize, saying their work was substandard and any good that came from it was thanks to the team. Western employers will not read this as appropriate humility. They'll take a worker at his word that he could have done better. Constantly apologizing and refusing to accept praise has held many back from advancing their careers.

Managers and colleagues need to see that you are doing good work. This is true at every level. During one meeting, I observed a new senior executive who had recently joined the company. One male member of my staff was quite effective at drawing out questions and giving answers that highlighted his intelligence and abilities, impressing this individual. A female staff member also fielded questions, but her answers were so brief and to the point that they appeared to the executive to be unremarkable, as though drawn from a pool of common knowledge. When the meeting was over, the executive commented to me about the male staff member. I went out of my way to assure him that the woman, who because of her modesty had been overlooked, was also knowledgeable and highly skilled.

If I had not been at the meeting, would anyone else have highlighted her strong points? Probably not, as no one would have been in a position to do so. Having an executive sponsor can make all the difference when it comes to getting the credit you deserve. I have benefited greatly by having senior managers speak up on my behalf. This opened many doors in my early career, including giving me the opportunity to transition from IT to the business team. Executive sponsors staked their credibility on my performance, securing my gratitude and loyalty. Some of them were not even in the chain of command I reported to.

By all means, seek out people who can help you, wherever in your company they may be. Make cultivating your positive relationships with them a daily priority. However, do not rely completely on others when it comes to highlighting your qualities. When offered praise, say thank you, and when you see an opportunity to let people know what you can do, take it. Don't brag; simply be honest about your abilities. This gives superiors the chance to observe you in the best light. They need to see your individual merits, not just the team's, to know that you are ready to advance.

Remembering that your brand is not your team will help you put emphasis on personal achievement. Nothing is wrong with praising your team. When you direct attention to group accomplishments, you build team spirit. However, beware of the tendency to give away so much credit that none is left for yourself. People judge your worth based on what they see you doing, not on what your team has done. This implies the need for repeated reminders of why you are the right person to lead. If you fail to highlight your energetic leadership and personal contribution to company growth, your superiors will wonder what role you play on the team. When opportunities to promote from within arise, they'll look elsewhere. Never take it for granted that as long as your team is doing well, the company will view you as indispensable.

When a machine works well, people don't notice its parts. The same is true of a well-managed team. Only when work breaks down are supervisors sure to pay attention. Ask yourself: Would a person looking at my team from the outside notice the individual achievements of its members, including me? Could someone easily identify the contributions I make, both in terms of hard skills and soft? Perhaps your management style lifts other people up. That is good, even essential, for the team to do its best work. But if all credit for team projects goes to the group, observers won't be able to spot individual strengths that may qualify a person for promotion. If your strengths are not on display, it might look to your employers like anybody could do your job.

How can you avoid this predicament? When it comes time to show off deliverables, be sure to point out creative solutions, briefly identifying the team member whose insight made that solution possible. Don't recite a laundry list—people zone out quickly if a report becomes too technical—but try to cite at least one person who deserves individual praise. During or after you have done this, make sure you mention challenges you issued to the team, then praise them for rising to the occasion. This emphasizes your role as organizer. If the deliverable was especially complex, requiring you to put in long hours or use unconventional motivating tactics, point this out. Learning to balance praising the team with taking personal credit will take time. Don't make the mistake of thinking it is less important than other executive skills. Changes in corporate oversight or direction can strike like a hurricane. The next time one happens at your company, having a strong personal brand may make the difference between staying in place or being swept away.

Since your goal is to make a name for yourself, make efforts to stand out from the crowd. My time at Merck gave me an opportunity to do this by showcasing my fashion sense. The color palette in corporate America at the time was drab, to put it mildly. How many black suits, gray suits, and dark blue suits can one person have? Enough to make it through the work week, apparently. Walking through the halls of the company, I felt like I was a black-and-white movie.

One day I decided to change things up. I picked out a modest, businesslike outfit from my wardrobe. Its color was candy apple red. That happened to be a slow morning in the IT department, so I didn't get seen much outside the office before noon. Merck wanted its employees to be a happy family, so cafeteria lunches were part of everyone's daily schedule. When I passed through the door of the cafeteria that day, the clatter of forks on plates fell silent. People were more stunned than shocked, I think. I mean, it's not like I was wearing something scandalous. They were just like, "Wow. Color!" Nobody knew what to say.

I'm not going to claim that my appearance revolutionized corporate culture or anything. I didn't appear on the cover of *Fortune 500* as the lady in the red dress. My point is that raising your profile at work isn't only about job performance. Showing some personality can be a big help. Think of it this way: If two similar candidates were up for a promotion and you were asked to make the call, would you be more likely to give the nod to an anonymous stranger or to a person who was known to you by name, or even nickname? Part of managing perception is helping others picture the future. After my cafeteria debut, my colleagues at Merck had an answer to the question, "Ivy who?" Had I wanted to extend my stay after graduation, it would have been easier for them to imagine having me around.

Maintaining a positive personal brand is one of the most difficult challenges of an executive position. It involves part marketing, part people skills, and part natural talent. Success depends on many factors, and effective strategies vary with the situation. However, no matter what conditions you find yourself in, you must make a daily effort to distinguish yourself in a leadership role. Think about each member of your team. What do you know about the role each one plays? Look at other leaders in your organization. Can you see the impact their guidance has on the people they lead?

In an earlier chapter I mentioned my cousin Roger, who was frustrated at being denied promotions he felt he deserved. Being overlooked was especially hard for Roger, I suspect, because he comes from a remarkable family. His brothers Peter and Lee have both had great success in their disparate fields. In part, this is due to the consistency of the way each man approaches life.

Cousin Peter is famous for his fearlessness. He never worries about what others think of him or what society says he should be doing with his time and his money. A risk taker, he has put his fortune on the line multiple times, lost it all, and built it back to greater heights. I have long admired his boldness, though I can't exactly empathize. My personality directs me to take calculated risks. It is one thing to look at a situation where you know all the variables and can weigh every outcome before deciding to act. It is another to see a door that you have no idea what's behind and open it. That is the sort of risk I never take. Cousin Peter flings every door open wide.

During a tough time in my own career, I asked him why he pushes ahead when so many other people would hold back. He answered by issuing a challenge.

"What could you do if you had no fear?"

Fear places a limit on accomplishment, and in Peter's mind, any limit is unacceptable. He sums up the secret to his success in a single word, "Audacity." Following his fearless outlook has made it possible for him to ride the economic tide.

My other cousin, Lee, worked for years as a software engineer in Silicon Valley. After a company he was a part of held an IPO, he found himself financially set for life. But Lee is not motivated primarily by money. His passion is pushing the boundaries of technology. Soon after the IPO, he founded a new company with high-tech goals. Eventually, that company too went public. Though Lee's outlook is different from Peter's, he overcomes technical challenges with his own form of audacity. He never accepts that anything he wants to do is impossible.

My cousins Roger, Peter, and Lee are examples I strive to follow in many ways. The way they manage their respective brands is only one of them. In this are—as in my career in general—I have found that people are most successful when they honestly examine their strengths and do what they are passionate about. If you can do the work you have now audaciously, success is assured. If you can find a way to make your passion your work, you'll have taken a huge step toward reaching your potential. Where do you see yourself in ten years? What risks would you take to get there in half the time?

A practical way to accelerate your progress is to volunteer for special projects that may have little to do with your current job. At one time, I realized I could benefit from knowing what it was like to work in a customer call center. A project came along that would permit me to work closely with people on the call service floor. I jumped at the chance. Another position I had my eye on required a strong understanding of profit and loss statements. During a planning meeting for a new project, I nominated myself to manage the budget. There were more experienced accountants in the room, but because my career plan called for mastering skills outside my comfort zone, I forced myself to put in the extra effort.

Time is money, so taking on work you haven't yet been trained for or don't strictly speaking "have to" do is risky behavior. When I advise mentees to have a giving attitude, I sometimes evoke a cringe. Nobody wants to be saddled with added responsibilities when benefits are not guaranteed. Men especially, in my experience, are unwilling to make this sort of sacrifice. Congratulations, ladies! Here's something that comes easier to us than it does to them. Women tend to be givers by nature. Following my own inclination has led me to discover that people who give willingly get more in return.

I have also learned that we do not always know the full significance of what we do for others. When I left my VP position at QVC, the team presented me with a book they'd put together. It contained notes from people I had helped over the years, all talking about the impact I'd had on their lives. In several cases, I am embarrassed to say, I did not remember the precise incident. I did what I did at the time because I thought it was the right thing to do. My actions took little effort and were simple, from my perspective. Looking at the book showed me that kindness and support of others creates a ripple effect. Their lives are improved, often in ways we cannot anticipate, and that puts them in a position to pass positivity on to others. My point is, you never know what the downstream benefits of your generosity will be, so don't hold back.

Ask yourself, "Will giving a little more time and energy now help me get a lot back later?" Keeping your end goal in mind will help you think long term. Working for the betterment of the company and your team will help you polish your personal brand to a high gloss. And the risk is not too high. You can't go into debt by giving your all, and it is better to be known as too generous than greedy with your time. In the advertising world, brands can be classified by the audience they target. Products are said to belong to "prestige brands" when owning them confers a certain cachet. Are employers eager to own your personal brand?

I have striven to build my brand on work ethic, authentic leadership, tenacity, integrity, and trust. When I commit, I always deliver. I make my decisions in the pursuit of honor. Managing perception has meant, for me, ensuring that others can see the positive qualities motivating my actions. I am not superhuman. I do not have more hours in the day than anybody else. Success in my executive positions has come from applying the power of my mind.

Chapter Nine

Live Like There's No Tomorrow

From the age of six to my middle teens, I was trained by a series of teachers in classical piano. I didn't hate the lessons, but sometime in my high school years, I developed the habit of pushing back at everything I didn't choose for myself. The competitions Mom put me in were stressful, so I decided I wanted out. As soon as I became stubborn enough to stand up to Mom's disapproval, I stopped playing piano cold. No more lessons. No competitions. I didn't even practice.

Back then, I thought that if I ever wanted to take up playing for myself, the ability would be waiting there for me. Any musicians reading this book, learn from my mistake. Habit keeps your skills in top shape, and it takes much more effort to get back into a good habit than it does to keep it up. As a professional, as well as a wife and mother, I find it hard to imagine having the time to take up piano again. If I could talk to teenage Ivy right now, I'd tell her to sit down and practice her scales. The competitions could go, but losing an interesting skill that could be enriching my life today wasn't worth scoring points off Mom.

To give myself credit, I haven't always hidden my lamp under a bushel. Mom didn't cook, so at a young age, I took it on myself to learn Chinese cooking. It became a hobby that built my confidence in myself. I got pretty good, but my parents wouldn't consider letting me go to culinary school. In our culture, chefs are looked down on as humble service workers. My interest in dance got even less traction at home. Mom and Dad tolerated the arts, but too much movement in that direction they considered a waste of energy. When my dance instructor told me I had potential, my parents reminded me that I needed to focus on academics in order to become a doctor or engineer. Later, I met several teachers who were willing to broaden my horizons. Thanks to them, I have come to believe that anyone can be successful in whatever role they choose in life. The key is to strike while the iron is hot. If you put off pursuing your goals until the future, the opportunities that were once available may be gone. Years ago, I had a nightmare that I only had one month to live. Ever since, I've been driven to do what I can with the time I have left. Though I hope to count that time in decades, taking the perspective that I may not have a tomorrow has pushed me to live life to the fullest today.

The role of parents, in my opinion, is to expose our children to as many different experiences as soon as possible. Having walked many paths ourselves, we are equipped to unlock doors and shine lights down alleys, as well as block those paths we know to be dangerous. My husband and I encourage our kids to show us what they're curious about. We've been blessed with opportunities to vacation in different countries. Exposing the kids to a variety of lifestyles has been invaluable in our efforts to cultivate their interests. It's fascinating to watch their interests branching off, sometimes diverting quite sharply from mine.

Remembering my mixed emotions about the piano, I talked my husband into letting Emily try a few lessons before we signed her to a lengthy commitment. When she didn't take to it at first, we decided not to make her continue. When she got a little older, she surprised me by asking to start back with her lessons. This was the best possible outcome. In the Chinese community I grew up in, parents constantly obsessed over anything their kids could compete over, like my dreaded piano competitions. It was a joy to see Emily take on something without pressure from me or Bernie.

Of course, we do apply pressure when necessary. In my own teenage years, my parents told me that my only job was to get good grades in school. I think now that this advice did me a disservice. There are soft skills not taught in classrooms that will serve people throughout their careers. That is why I advise parents to encourage teenage children to get a part-time job. But not just any job. The teenager's end goal should not be only to make money but to gain experience in life, to learn by doing. Thus, they need to seek work that aligns with their long-term goals. The sooner we can help them find their interests, the sooner they can walk the path to success.

The similar ways I talk about family and working life is no accident. In my experience, the skills that help you achieve at home are equally beneficial around the office. I have learned much about patience from being a mother. My children don't always act the way I would in a given situation. Forcing them to do things my way has never brought long-lasting positive results. Bearing this in mind, I don't expect bossing my adult team members around to have a better outcome. Advising, correcting, and suggesting we try another way has proved more productive in both settings.

Please consider another example. Parents and team leaders must be careful not to focus on negatives. When you see your child's report card, do you skip over the As in favor of criticizing the Bs, Cs, or Ds? People who set their sights on perfection often pass over good work that deserves praise. Criticism without praise feels like persecution. When reviewing a report card, it is important to accentuate the positive. The same holds true when inspecting team achievements. If you only see failures, how will you build on strengths? Even when improvement is necessary, don't forget to give praise when you can.

Growing up, I was taught that the goal of parents should be to store up money to pass on to the next generation. I had to learn on my own the importance of investing in yourself. You have to enjoy life along the way, or else what is living for? Too many of my older relatives spent all their lives saving, expecting to check items off their bucket lists after they retired. Often their lives took a turn that made this impossible. Ill health, financial difficulties, or a combination of both wrecked their plans.

It is a sad irony that so many generations have grown up believing they must live first for their parents (Excel at school! Become independent!), then for their children (Save up for college! Give a boost to adult life!), and finally for their parents again (Hand over your paycheck!). When does anyone in that cycle have time to live their own life?

It is better to live every day like there is no tomorrow. Don't wait to attack your bucket list. Give yourself permission to live now so that when your time has come to leave this world, you have no regrets. Reviewing my school days, my time in university, and my early career for this book have reminded me of many people whose generosity and wisdom made me who I am. To thank them all would require many more pages, but it is not necessary, because I make it a policy to express my gratitude on a regular basis. This both cements the bonds I have and saves me from much self-doubt, as I will explain.

Eventually, we all must face the loss of colleagues, friends, and family members in death. The negative thoughts and emotions of such an experience are unique, but an effective strategy for dealing with them is to communicate with loved ones proactively, not letting an opportunity to express your feelings slip by. Positive thinking and a bold taste for new experiences can help transform grief into a burden you can bear, but if you have not prepared yourself by being open with people you love or admire, the finality of death can be overwhelming. None of us knows when we may be seeing someone for the last time. This means we must optimize every moment.

About four years ago I attended a funeral for a former coworker at QVC. Also in attendance was a CIO who had been helpful to me while I was with the company. We greeted each other and spoke about our colleague and old times. Because of the somber occasion, it was easy to remember the importance of taking time to say what was important. I told my friend how much I appreciated his support. He had been a lamppost lighting my way, so before we parted, I thanked him for the blessings his kindness had brought me. A month later, I heard he had passed away. I was saddened at his loss but grateful we'd been able to talk.

My father wasn't a man who applauded little victories. I rarely heard him say, "Good job." Maybe that was because he set such high standards for himself, or maybe it was a holdover from his own strict upbringing. Whatever the reason, it didn't make me love him any less. Far from it. I am thankful for his influence on my upbringing and the sacrifices he made on my behalf. When his ninetieth birthday approached, I decided to do something special. A man doesn't reach his ninth decade without his fair share of health problems, so I knew there were important people Dad might not have another chance to see in life. I set a goal to throw him a party that would create new memories and shine a light on favorite old ones. I researched his nearest and dearest and cast a wide net, inviting friends and relatives Dad had not seen in years. Several were practically strangers to me.

Some guests had long distances to travel. The trip would be expensive for some, so I made plans early and let everybody know the date and place well in advance. I went at the challenge of organizing and promoting the occasion like I would have an important event in my professional life. In the end, relatives from both the US and Taiwan came together to visit Dad in his home. He spent his day reminiscing and reconnecting with family and friends. Everybody had a memorable time.

About five months later I was on a flight from Charlotte, NC, to Philadelphia. Dad called in the middle of the flight to tell me he'd had a heart attack. He was on his way to the hospital and didn't know what the outcome would be. Since I was in the air when he made the call, I didn't hear any of this until I checked my messages on the ground. By the time I got a knowledgeable person on the phone, Dad was gone. I was sad, of course, but I thought back to our last big day, the reunion on Dad's ninetieth, when we'd all been together. Afterward he had given me a rare, "Good job." I had felt at the time that seeing different generations of our family interact was thanks enough. In my changed circumstances, his appreciation meant even more.

Don't let important moments pass you by. Be prepared to go beyond words. Show people you care about how you feel. Don't wait for a chance meeting or special event. Two years back I got a call from a relative, who said my uncle had passed. His wife, Mom's sister, had been dependent on my uncle for many years. Now that he was gone, the family was making arrangements for the funeral and to take care of my aunt. Since family members know I am a busy person, they did not make unreasonable demands, but simply asked that I be present over the weekend. Of course I agreed, flying out to San Francisco ASAP.

My relationship with my aunt is not all candy and flowers. When I was little, I used to stay with her in Hong Kong. She was a strict person, not the kind to get down on a kid's level. I remember when she took one look at the beautiful long hair I loved so much and said, "We'll have to get you a haircut. Long hair attracts lice." Whatever protests I offered didn't work, because our next stop was the salon, where my hair was trimmed to shoulder length. All this was in the past, of course, so when I stepped off the plane in California, I was determined to do what I could for her. However, on that day, a call came through that disturbed my peace of mind. Aunty Irene, the woman who had looked after me during high school, had died. She'd been living on an island near Boston, Massachusetts, about as far from my location as was possible to get without leaving the country.

Coping with that news was a real challenge to me. Unlike with Dad, I couldn't point to one special day that summed up all I'd done to let Aunty Irene know I cared. Her example had been such a huge influence on the person I am that I wondered if I had done enough to express my feelings. For a few crazy minutes, I tried to figure out if there was a way I could get back across the country in time for her funeral. There wasn't. Besides, what good would it have done? The person I wanted to talk to was Aunty Irene, and she was beyond my reach.

I sat down and thought through my grief. Had I left things unsaid? No. The gifts I've been given in life and the lessons I have learned move me to live like there's no tomorrow. Every day I work to eliminate stress and unhappiness for others. Part of the way I do this is by giving praise to those around me and letting loved ones know I care. Aunty Irene had been close enough to my inner circle that I was confident she felt appreciated. The shock of her death had made me doubt, but this was not a rational reaction. I had given time in plenty to Aunty Irene, and time is a precious gift to anyone. It is especially valuable to older persons. Remembering this helped me to get past my doubts. I was sure that if I could have talked to Aunty Irene right before the end, she would have told me that she knew where we stood. She was a great lady and a wonderful friend.

Losing Aunty Irene at a time when I could not share my grief with her nearest and dearest seemed unfair. To move past this sense of injustice, I remembered a strategy taught to me by my good friend Faye. A deeply spiritual person, Faye has made a study of world religions. Buddhist teachings in particular are a great comfort to her. Despite her many virtues, she has suffered much in life. I once asked how she endures with such grace. She explained that much of the frustration people struggle with is caused by a feeling that since bad things happen to good people, the universe is out of balance.

According to Faye, this belief is due to a narrow point of view. Those frustrated by suffering think only of this life. Yet life, Faye told me, is cyclical. We travel a path from birth to death, then return to birth in a new form. The life we have now is only a small part of a greater whole, a line of simple poetry in an epic play. When bad things happen to us, can we truly blame the universe? Perhaps we are paying for bad we did in a previous life. Rather than presenting us with imbalance, the universe is offering us a chance to level the scales.

The idea that we live in a balanced universe where justice is as fundamental as mathematics appeals to me, but Faye's belief comes with a caution. When we experience unhappiness in this life, it's natural to hold grudges and take out our bad feelings on others. Think about the effect that has on the balanced universe! By letting negativity motivate us, we can add to the debt of evil we have to pay back, either in this life or another. To escape from suffering, we must accept that we have debts to pay. We must let our sense of injustice go and allow trials to refine our personalities.

Reminding myself that my perspective is limited help me set aside negative feelings and support my flesh-and-blood aunt. I made a choice to optimize the moment with the people in front of me. A small gathering of Aunty Irene's family and friends gathered on that weekend without me. A month later, I was able to attend a larger gathering where I spoke publicly about how Aunty Irene touched my heart. I told my listeners that I planned to keep her legacy alive. She had always supported me when I needed understanding. On that day, I renewed my resolve to imitate her empathy.

If you want to live a happy life, you must live without regret. Maximize each day for yourself and make sure the people you care about know you appreciate them. There comes a day for everyone when there is no tomorrow. Leave nothing undone you should have done, nothing unsaid your soul wanted to say. I remind myself to live this way each day, so that when I have seen my final sunset, I can leave this life behind in peace.

Chapter Ten

Your Journey Is Ahead of You

Our natural human tendency is to think in extremes. Hot and cold. Night and day. East and west. We imagine ourselves navigating between opposites, finding the middle path that will skirt around whirlpools and bring us safely to our destination. Most of the forces we wrestle with in life can be thought of in this way. Work and family both give us purpose. At times, these purposes can appear to conflict. If we are to achieve our greatest potential, we must find a way for them to act in harmony.

My brief but accomplished musical career acquainted me with the consonant and dissonant chords. When played simultaneously, the tension between these opposites resolves with an audible release that is pleasing to the ear. Tension in life can do the same if you apply the right kind of pressure. Piano keys pressed by the fingers strike resonant wires. In life, pressure comes from all around. Tradition is a form of pressure, as is reason. The advantage of reason is that it is flexible. Like a pianist's trained hands, it can be harnessed to sound the right notes.

Many of the ideas in this book were taught to me by mentors. Others I worked out on my own using the processes I described. When I think back over the journey of my life, I realize the power of my mind has produced the greatest harmony and thus been responsible for my success. In high school, creative thinking got me over the mountain that was English. At Drexel University, my mind's ability to organize helped me step into a leadership role. As I transitioned into full-time working life, forming a mental picture of the future enabled me to focus on soft skills I needed to excel as head of my department, then in various executive roles.

Is my mind the exception or the rule? I occasionally get the impression from people who ask me for advice that they believe success is a birthright, a talent someone either does or does not have. Or if not a birthright, then a secret, something only successful people know. I can tell you from experience that there is no secret. Everyone has strengths and anyone can succeed. If you can find your strength and apply your mind to making the world better, you will be successful.

If there is a difference between myself and my peers, it's my faith. I have faith in the impulse that saved my life and led me to my husband. I have faith in my purpose, even though I'm not 100% sure what it is. I have faith that the universe favors balance over imbalance, order over chaos, and that if I don't run up life debts, I'll be better off in the long run. By focusing on the positive end, writing down my goals and strengths and passions, and telling people how they can support the success I want to achieve, I position my physical self to receive their help. But I am more than my physical self. My mind and heart are intangible. They are part of the universe. Only by opening my mind and heart to the universe can I channel its power.

When our eyes see the light of a distant star, we're receiving a signal that was broadcast from so far away we can't truly comprehend the distance. That signal is lovely but random, so far as science can tell us. The signals we broadcast to the universe are far more meaningful. They connect us with opportunities and individuals who can help us align with our purposes in life. I know that not everybody is comfortable talking about faith. We all have different experiences that shape our views. I'm not going to insist you have faith in my philosophy, or even in me.

I only ask that you have faith in one thing. Have faith that if you apply your mind to a matter, you will succeed. This is not a passive faith; you have to live it. In every situation, you must exercise the power of the mind. Think through problems from different perspectives. Don't restrict yourself to traditional solutions. Don't reject solutions simply because they are traditional. Don't allow fear to get between you and your end goal, and don't limit yourself to working for immediate, obvious rewards. When you're challenged to try something new, don't hold back because you're afraid to fail. "Be audacious!" as my cousin Peter said. Give freely and you will receive.

Many people I have worked with over the years have been limited in their personal success because they did not think things through, merely reacting to events. Others I have known were held back by concentrating too heavily on one part of their life plan when other aspects needed attention. Some excelled at hard skills but lacked the basic soft skills to get ahead. Others adopted traditional or cultural modes of behavior without considering their appropriateness to the circumstance. These are all mistakes that could have been avoided with a dose of radical thinking and focusing on the positive end.

Perhaps you are struggling to decide what you want in life. Everyone wants to be happy. Start with that. Use the power of your mind to dissect happiness, discovering what it means to you. How can you get from where you are to where you're going? Here's a hint. If the step-by-step plan you come up with looks like a list of things you want other people to do for you, it won't help you achieve your goal. In all likelihood, it will bring you back to your starting point, no wiser than when you began. Don't plan for others to help you. Plan to help others. The more you give, the more you get. The universe pays back its debts.

When all is said and done, the power of your mind will accomplish your greatest tasks. The only limit is the size of your dreams. So think big. Dream big. Tasks are only impossible until somebody does them. Don't get trapped in the same old, same old. Innovate! Challenge yourself to get out of your comfort zone. Write down your achievements. Take a pic a day. Don't get upset about disagreements you won't remember in three days. Plan for the future, then live each day as if it's your last. It's your life. Live it. Believe without limits, and you can think your way to your full potential.

About the Author

Ivy Chin is a senior executive with more than twenty-five years of experience. She has implemented groundbreaking e-commerce strategies in support of popular American retailers. Her rare blend of technology and business expertise has made her an innovator, while her grounded approach and creativity have brought a sense of fun to the challenge of leading a team.

After graduating from Drexel University in Philadelphia, PA, with a bachelor's degree in computer science, she found success in multiple business and technical roles, beginning with a term of service at CertainTeed Corporation. Seeing new opportunities in the early days of the Internet, she joined QVC, Inc., eventually serving as vice president for QVC.com. Thanks to initiatives she helped pioneer, web sales grew immensely during her tenure. Among many other achievements at QVC.com, she was instrumental in the website's user experience being ranked one of the best online.

Following this success, she joined Belk, Inc. as senior vice president of eCommerce. At Belk, she led upward of 120 web merchandising, creative, operations, and marketing staff, accelerating online retail growth. Sales at belk.com grew rapidly during her tenure, bringing profitability to the platform well ahead of projections. Hand-selected by Belk's CEO to participate in multiple mission-critical projects, she became a two-time recipient of the William Belk Award, the company's highest honor. Later, as a senior vice president for PetSmart, she advised on digital strategy and optimized business operations.

Several journals have recognized her abilities and achievements in the industry. Among the lists that have included her name are "Top 10 Women in Retail Tech" from *Chain Store Age*, "Top 50 Women" from *Multi-Channel Retailing*, and "Premier 100 IT Leaders" from *Computerworld*. She received a "Women in Business Award" from the *Charlotte Business Journal* and an "Alumni Circle of Distinction Award" from Drexel University's College of Engineering. She is most proud of her "Committed to the Success of Our Associates Award," as voted on by Belk employees.

Ivy credits her upbringing, her mentors, her managers, and her teams, as well as the support of her loving family and friends, for their contributions to her achievements. Above all, she acknowledges that success has come about thanks to the power of her mind.

Made in the USA
Middletown, DE
17 July 2018